BRITAIN A COUNTRY COMPASS

AN ENCHANTING WORLD OF SIGHTS AND SOUNDS

Previous page:
Spring in the alpine meadow at Wisley Garden, Surrey

This page:
Summer wheatfields on the downs near Alfriston, Sussex

Contents page:
Autumn in East Anglia: Thetford Warren, Norfolk

Introductory page:
North Hampshire parkland in the grip of winter

BRITAIN A COUNTRY COMPASS

AN ENCHANTING WORLD OF SIGHTS AND SOUNDS

AA

Produced by the Publications Division of the
Automobile Association

Editorial Consultant *Phil Drabble*

Text by *Diana Winsor, Michael Cady.* Editor *Michael
Cady.* Art Editor *Bob Johnson.* Editorial Assistants
Gail Harada, Richard Powell, Rebecca Snelling. Wildlife
illustrations by *Richard Draper* and
Ann Winterbotham. Geological map by
Geoff Jennings (FD Graphics)

Phototypeset by Tradespools Ltd, Frome,
Somerset, England
Printed and bound by New Interlitho SPA, Milan,
Italy

Published by The Automobile Association
Fanum House, Basingstoke, Hampshire
RG21 2EA

Contents

Introduction

Britain – A Country Compass introduces and describes many of the most fascinating aspects of the British countryside. The book opens with a description of the 'bones' of the landscape – the geological structures which give shape and variety to the countryside – from the flat expanses of East Anglia's fenlands to the austere mountain ranges of the Scottish Highlands. *The Hand of Man*, the next part of the book, tells the story of man's impact on the natural landscape, and shows how he has dramatically altered the British countryside. *The Living Countryside* is the main part of the book. In it are described and illustrated many of the habitats, sights and activities which make up the countryside. These range from ancient woodlands to estuaries and from cottage gardens to rural crafts. The last part of the book, *A Country Pathfinder*, includes a selected gazetteer of places to visit and lists societies and organizations to join, as well as giving hints on what to do and take to make the countryside more enjoyable.

A Note on the Wildlife Illustrations

Several vivid wildlife illustrations appear in the *The Living Countryside* part of the book. In them the artists have depicted various aspects of the countryside in a highly individualistic way. They depict plants and animals which may be seen in specific habitats; for example downlands, rivers and hedges. Some of the creatures can only be seen at certain times of the year, and not all the flowers shown bloom at the same time.

Foreword

To appreciate the British countryside to the full it is important to know not only what to look for and where to look, but to understand the reasons why the landscape developed as it did. The purpose of this book then is to light up the many paths a reader can take to discover the richness of Britain's rural inheritance – its solitude and wilderness, its mountain scenery and seascapes, its farmland and villages and its craftsmen.

The book also explores the history of the countryside. Created partly by the hand of man, many of Britain's cherished landscapes are the result of thousands of years of gradual change and dramatic upheaval. Though most of its forests have been cleared over the centuries to give way to prairies of ploughland or open moors, there still remains the vast patchwork of little fields and woods and copses, usually created neither for profit nor for pride, but often merely to provide cover for sportsmen to pursue their prey.

It is vital to strike a balance between the needs and ambitions of different – and perhaps conflicting – interests. If our children's children are to be left a heritage to be as proud of as we are, we must preserve the simple pleasures of the countryside, so that future generations may share in them too.

Phil Drabble

The Rocks Beneath

Great Britain has a total area of only 121,000 square miles, yet within this small area is found a great variety of scenery which is directly related to the underlying rock. Rock type affects not only scenery but also the occupations and livelihood of the inhabitants of an area; the soil and vegetation, the presence or absence of minerals and the number of roads and railways.

The geological time scale shown alongside the map divides rocks into groups according to the way in which they were formed and, secondly, according to their age. There are three main types of rock formation: igneous, sedimentary and metamorphic. For the purposes of this map, these are subdivided according to age and type into 15 categories. The numbers given after the terms below relate to the fifteen colours explained in the key and used to distinguish different geological areas of the map.

The word 'rock' generally suggests something very hard and solid, but in geology it is used to describe any substance making up the outer surface of the earth or crust, i.e. sand and clay are as much 'rocks' as hard granite.

Igneous Rocks (1) and (2)

The term 'igneous' is derived from the Latin *ignis* meaning fire, and all such rocks were formed from the molten lava which still makes up the core or centre of the earth. From time to time parts of the earth's crust move, releasing pressure on the material beneath the crust and allowing the hot molten material to escape either on to the surface, as volcanoes of various types, or into the outer layers of the crust. There the material cools to form part of the crust.

The material which cools beneath the surface, known as *intrusive* or *plutonic* rock (1), does so slowly and this allows gradual crystal formation, the results of which can often be seen with the naked eye in rocks such as granite and gabbro. These rocks contain many varied minerals including feldspar, quartz, biotite and mica, and the way in which these are combined gives the various rock names. Usually these rocks are extremely hard and are only exposed on the surface of the earth after thousands of years of weathering of rocks lying above them.

Molten materials which have found their way on to the surface cool much more rapidly, and as a result the crystals making up the rock are too small to be seen with the naked eye. Rocks formed in this way are known as *volcanic* rocks (2), and include basalt and andesite. Although there are no active volcanoes in Great Britain today, in the past great volcanic eruptions did occur, forming some of the highest parts of the country such as the mountains of Snowdonia, the Lake District and parts of Scotland.

Sedimentary Rocks (3) to (13)

During certain periods of geological history, parts of Britain were covered by the sea. River-borne silt and mud, together with the remains of dead sea creatures and plants, gradually accumulated on the sea bed, forming the sediments that eventually give rise to *sedimentary* rocks. By their own weight these materials, which occur in layers known as *strata*, are eventually compressed into rock. Sands form sandstones, sea creatures form chalk and limestone, and muds produce mudstone (shales).

Similarly, vegetation in swamp areas just above sea level produces dead plants which accumulate to form a peat-like material. Should this material be submerged by the sea and compacted by its own weight and that of overlying material it may become coal. In the hot equatorial climate of the Carboniferous period in Great Britain such swamps of giant ferns and club-mosses flourished and sedimentary rocks of the Coal Measures were formed in shallow seas or lakes.

In Britain today the remains or imprints (fossils) of creatures living in the sea millions of years ago are found in some mountains and hills, e.g. fossil sea urchins in the limestones of the Cotswolds, which lived in warm waters about 160 million years ago. The sediments in which these fossils are found have been slowly lifted from the sea bed, contorted and tipped as the earth has cooled and shrunk during four main periods of Britain's geological history. At these times the British Isles gradually took on the shape they have today.

The oldest sedimentaries (3) are found in the Shetland Islands, whilst Pre-Cambrian and Cambrian sedimentaries (3 and 4) are found along the Welsh borders in Caer Caradoc and the Malvern Hills as well as the Grampians of Scotland. It is within these rocks that the first fossils appear in abundance in the form of Trilobites.

Parts of the Southern Uplands and the mountains of Wales, made up mainly of shales and mudstones, were raised in Ordovician times (5) and their rocks contain abundant Graptolite and Trilobite fossils.

Fifty million years later, at the end of the Silurian period (6), the materials which had been collecting in the shallow waters covering much of Britain, particularly primitive coral reefs and sea lilies (crinoids) and later mud, were folded up to form the surface outcrops at Wenlock Edge.

For the next 50 million years, during the Devonian period (7), much of Great Britain became dry land, worn down by weathering, in dry conditions with occasional periods of heavy rain. Pebbles, sand and mud gathered in small basins, temporary lakes and coastal deltas. The sea extended in a line from northern Devon and Cornwall across Britain to the Ardennes. In clear areas of shallow sea coral reefs flourished and limestone-forming deposits accumulated.

During the Carboniferous period (8) the sea gradually encroached northwards, lapping round mountains already formed in Wales and north Scotland. For millions of years lime-bearing muds accumulated in shallow clear waters, later to form Carboniferous limestone. In deeper parts of the sea sand and coarser black muds accumulated. By the end of the period the sea had silted up and delta and estuary conditions existed over northern England and southern Scotland in which sand and mud accumulated. Lush swamp vegetation grew on the mud flats – later to form the coal mentioned earlier. The end of the Carboniferous period was marked by strong earth movements; rocks formed earlier were warped up to form high land particularly in the area of the Pennines.

During Permian and Triassic times (9) and (10) the climate of Britain was akin to a desert and wide expanses of sand dunes were formed by easterly winds. Material produced by weathering, including angular rocks and gravel, was swept into basins by temporary rivers. Only for one relatively brief period during the Permian age did the sea invade a part of Britain, when an arm of shallow sea from Europe spread into a part of northern England east of the Pennines. In this sea a series of magnesian limestones and marls were formed. In late Triassic times large quantities of salty water which periodically dried up to form rock salt lay across central Britain. The deposits were thickest in the area around Cheshire, which has produced salt commercially for centuries.

In Jurassic times (11) a shallow sea spread rapidly northward over southern Britain making islands of the already high areas. With fluctuations in sea level a variety of sedimentary rocks were laid down with muds, limestones and corals being most characteristic. The limestone produced during this period today forms one long – but not continuous – ridge from the North York Moors through the Cotswolds to the Isle of Purbeck. This ridge yields fine building stone and much iron ore. This limestone is made up of minute spheres of calcium carbonate, yellowish in colour and far less massive in structure than earlier Carboniferous limestone. These beds were subsequently tilted and now have a marked scarp (steep) slope generally facing north-west and particularly noticeable in the Cotswolds.

At the beginning of the Cretaceous period (12), with a slight change in sea level, much of southern England became an area of delta swamps into which rivers brought layers of sands and clays eroded from the lands further north and west, over a period of 35 million years. This was followed by a further incursion of a shallow sea from the east. In this sea lived minute

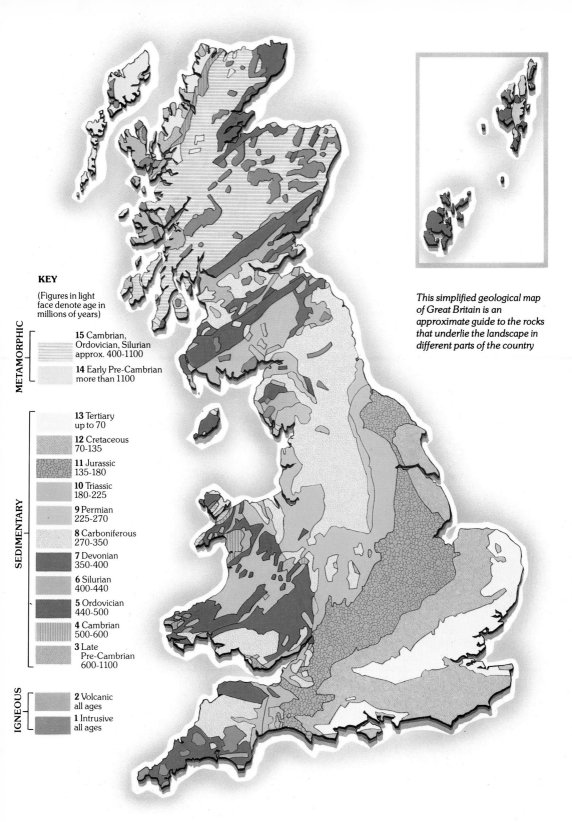

KEY

(Figures in light face denote age in millions of years)

METAMORPHIC

	15 Cambrian, Ordovician, Silurian approx. 400-1100	
	14 Early Pre-Cambrian more than 1100	

SEDIMENTARY

13 Tertiary up to 70

12 Cretaceous 70-135

11 Jurassic 135-180

10 Triassic 180-225

9 Permian 225-270

8 Carboniferous 270-350

7 Devonian 350-400

6 Silurian 400-440

5 Ordovician 440-500

4 Cambrian 500-600

3 Late Pre-Cambrian 600-1100

IGNEOUS

2 Volcanic all ages

1 Intrusive all ages

This simplified geological map of Great Britain is an approximate guide to the rocks that underlie the landscape in different parts of the country

sea creatures, sponges, corals and plants whose remains accumulated at a very slow rate on the sea bed. Flints (perhaps products of decomposition or impurities) within the chalk beds provided early man with tools. With minor fluctuations of sea level, changes in the material laid down occurred and layers of clay were also deposited. These deposits were later warped or folded to form the scarplands of southern England.

In Tertiary times (13), when these scarplands were formed by folding, the sea was able to invade from the east and rivers draining into it deposited pebbles, clay and sands from areas above sea level, which

were to form the London clay and the sands of Bagshot Heath and other regions.

By the end of the Tertiary period the British Isles were at last beginning to look as they do today and became completely dry land for the first time in millions of years with no deposition going on anywhere.

Metamorphic Rocks (14) and (15)
The term metamorphism means 'change'. During the stormy history of the British Isles not only were rocks being formed and uplifted, but volcanic activity and the movement of hot lava took place, which then produced new rock material, and

affected the surrounding rocks. In the case of folding, older rocks already compacted were often compacted further and as a result changed their form; many areas of shale formed originally from mud then became slate in areas such as Wales and the Lake District. Similarly, marble and gneiss are formed by the metamorphism by heat of limestone and granite respectively. These rocks are found chiefly in the old highland areas which have been subjected to heat and/or pressure over many millions of years and most are very ancient in origin. They form some of the hardest rocks and highest areas of the British Isles.

9

The Shape of the Land

NOWHERE else in the world is there so rich a diversity of geological formation within so small an area as in Britain. Within these islands are rocks of almost every age and composition, from the crystalline rocks of the Outer Hebrides to the crumbling white chalk of the South Downs. So many different physical forces have acted upon them over millions of years, buckling, eroding and adding to them, that they have produced a landscape of infinite variety.

In the beginning

At the beginning of the geological time scale the whole surface of the earth was undergoing volcanic turmoil. Lava spilled from every fissure. Molten rock solidified and crystallized under intense pressure beneath the cooling crust. Known as igneous rocks, from the Latin word for fire, these are the oldest rocks in Britain, whether in their original form like the black basalt layers around Fingal's Cave on the Island of Staffa and eroded peaks of Snowdonia, the Lake District and Scotland, or in even more ancient, but much altered form such as the red sandstone of Scotland's far north-western mountains and the gneiss strata of the Isle of Lewis.

All these uplands, once so turbulent and now so peaceful, were formed anything from 4,000 million to some 60 million years ago, and most of them pre-date any life on earth. They contain no fossils, only minerals. Translucent agates are found in the younger basalts; amethyst and the smoky quartz called Cairngorm in granite. The much-changed metamorphic rocks contain garnets, slate, serpentine and pockets of marble.

The first life on earth

It was in the mountains of Wales that fossil life was first discovered, and so the earliest rocks to contain such evidence of living organisms were called Cambrian, after the Celtic name for Wales. All that went before were known as Pre-Cambrian. The succeeding millennia were categorized as the Palaeozoic, Mesozoic, Cainozoic and Quaternary ages, or the first, second, third and fourth stages of life on earth. However, some geologists regard the Quaternary Age as a subdivision of the Cainozoic, thus reducing the number of stages to three.

Not that the Cambrian rocks of some 600 million years ago were any less violently formed. Volcanoes erupted, great seas moved and only the most primitive of creatures, trilobites and brachiopods among them, appeared in the liquid muds and steaming waters.

Britain did not exist as any kind of unified land mass when the first vertebrates appeared some 450 million years ago in the Ordovician and Silurian periods of the Palaeozoic Age. There was only a great sea, broken by the volcanic mountains

of the Pre-Cambrian age millions of years before. Over succeeding millennia, for another 100 million years or more, the great upland sediments of Silurian rocks that cover most of central and northern Wales and the Scottish border country were created out of sand, mud, and the coral limestones formed around the accumulating skeletons of untold billions of microscopic sea creatures. Vegetation, mostly mosses, gradually emerged.

Most abundant in the seas of the Devonian period that followed were fish, whose fossils can be found in the Old Red Sandstones of Cornwall, Devon, parts of south Wales, the west Midlands, central and north-eastern Scotland. It contains evidence too of ferns, reeds, fresh water, and giant moss trees flourishing in a moist, warm atmosphere, the beginnings of the Carboniferous period of about 300 million years ago, when increasing amounts of limestone, sandstone, shale and seams of coal and iron were laid down to underlie much of Britain's industrial areas today.

As the seas moved, the land emerged, and the great carboniferous forests of giant ferns, horsetails and other luxuriant ancestors of our most primitive plants spread across much of Britain. The first amphibians appeared in shallow rivers and the edges of the sea. On the land and in the air invertebrates such as spiders, millipedes, dragonflies and beetles swarmed and multiplied. The coal we burn today is the decayed distillation of those rank and humid forests which once soaked up the sun we share today, before the dryer, wind-blown millennia of the Permian period covered them with sand and marked the end of the first, or Palaeozoic Age.

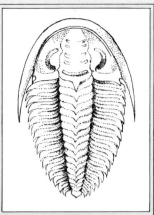

Fossils—trilobites
These marine animals lived in Palaeozoic times, and probably spent their lives crawling, swimming or lying half-buried in sediments on the sea-beds of the oceans which existed at that period. Trilobites have flattened bodies, almost oval in shape, and at first glance they resemble giant woodlice. They vary in length from an inch to a foot, and have a head, abdomen and small tail. The lower surfaces of trilobites, which are rarely visible in fossils, bear feathery extensions used for swimming and as gills for breathing. The trilobite in the illustration is *Callavia callavei*, which was abundant in Cambrian times.

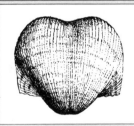

Fossils—brachiopods
Very numerous in Palaeozoic and Mesozoic times, brachiopods are found as fossils in most types of sediments which formed in shallow sea water. These soft-bodied animals were protected by a limy shell, and lived fixed to the sea floor by means of a muscular stalk. The body covering consisted of a double shell, made up of a lower half, or valve, in which the animal was contained, and an upper valve which acted as a cover. The valves were opened and closed by muscular action in order to take in food from the sea water. Fossil brachiopod shells are usually an inch or so across, and a number of different shapes and patterns of shell can be found. Some resemble in shape oil lamps used in ancient Rome, and for this reason are called lamp shells.

Snowdonia's Llanberis Pass, carved out of ancient rocks by a mighty glacier

The Shape of the Land

Dramatically folded rock formations at Stair Hole, Dorset. Lulworth Cove is in the background

Fossils—ammonites
The group of fossils known as ammonites, which range in size from a quarter of an inch to several feet in diameter, are the remains of the coiled and chambered shells of sea animals related to today's octopus. The animals floated in open water feeding on small invertebrates. When they died, the air in the chambers kept them afloat for some time before they sank to the sea bed. Ammonite fossils are common in the cliffs near Whitby, Yorkshire, and along the coast between Lyme Regis and Portland Bill in Dorset.

The age of the dinosaur

It is impossible to draw any fixed line between geological periods, but nevertheless the beginning of the Mesozoic Age does appear to mark a more stable time in the life of the earth. During the Triassic period plants began to change to more familiar forms. Much of England was covered in a great salt lagoon and the reptiles, the dinosaurs, began to dominate both land and sea, and later the air. The loamy marls and sandstones laid down in this period occupy roughly the area of that inland ocean – around the west Midlands with fragmented arms stretching south to the Devon coast, north to the Solway and the Yorkshire coast. These rocks contain fossil remains of such creatures as early crocodiles and the long-necked plesiosaurus, animals which continued to flourish and develop into the following Jurassic period of some 150 million years ago.

During the Jurassic period most of Europe lay beneath a coral sea studded with islands, its waters and shores crowded with often gigantic reptiles. The main bulk of Jurassic limestones form a great curving spine that swings north and east from the Dorset coast to Yorkshire, encompassing the grassy uplands of the Cotswolds where it provided the golden local stone. Curving to the south of the Jurassic limestone, often interlocking with it, is the soft white rock that defines the Cretaceous period of about 100 million years ago, the chalk of English downland. It appears in the Sussex and Wiltshire Downs, the Chilterns and the Lincolnshire wolds.

Chalk is also a lime-containing rock, composed chiefly of the shells of microscopic sea creatures. Contemporary with it are the Cretaceous clays and sandstones, which were laid down

not at the bottom of shallow seas, like chalk, but as sediment in the estuaries of great river deltas. On land in this period the huge ferns, conifers and horsetails were giving way to trees that we would recognize today – willows, oak and beech – through which moved such great animals as the iguanodon and the triceratops.

It was between the Cretaceous and the subsequent Eocene period that a great geological change took place, an upheaval of the earth's crust so fundamental that it was named Eocene, which comes from the Greek word *eos*, dawn: this was the dawn of the world as we know it today, and the beginning of the Cainozoic or third age.

In Britain, rocks of the Eocene and subsequent Oligocene and Pliocene periods of this third stage of geological time, and also from the Pleistocene Age which opened the era which has become the age of man, were formed mainly from sands, silts and clays. They began to be laid down about 50 million years ago in a world which had seen the last of the great reptiles and the beginning of a tremendous development among mammals. The climate was still warm, possibly sub-tropical in Britain, and plant and animal life thrived.

The Ice ages

During this period the climate began to change and it became much colder. About two million years ago, during the Pleistocene period, a massive glacier began to inch its way southward. In the end it was to cover most of Britain and northern Europe, and to lie thousands of feet thick.

The ice moved south over Britain at least four times, retreating only to return. Yet between such glaciations the climate improved, and because Britain was then part of the European land mass it was easy for plants and animals to recolonize the milder north. It was during one of these interglacial periods that man, too, appeared in Britain. About 150,000 years ago the skull of a man was embedded in the gravelly sediments of the Thames valley near the Kent village of Swanscombe. His skull is the earliest human fossil remain ever found in Britain. The ice reached as far as the Thames during the last glaciation about 20,000 years ago.

The breaking in of the sea just when it did to form the English Channel prevented certain species of animal and plant life from recolonizing Britain, and the Irish Sea proved an even more effective barrier between Britain and Ireland. But the sea also tempered the climate with a consistently milder, moister flow of air, encouraging the rapid growth of woodland over almost the whole country. The scene was then set for the arrival of modern man.

At Hunstanton Cliffs in Norfolk chalk overlays carstone

Fossils—corals
Although no living coral reefs are found in Britain, they still occur in some warm seas in other parts of the world. Australia's Great Barrier Reef is probably the best-known example. Coral is formed by millions of tiny animals whose external skeletons have contributed immensely to the formation of limestone areas such as Wenlock Edge in Shropshire, which in Silurian times was a coral reef almost 30 miles long. Some corals live solitary existences, but many live in colonies. The individual corals have a ribbed surface which is subdivided into irregular parts horizontally, and in cross section can be seen to have plates radiating out from the centre. Some coral groupings grow from a central stem and subdivide like the branches of a tree, while others are so tightly packed together that they become like six-sided honeycombs. Other corals have a chain-like structure, and many form rounded masses perforated with tiny holes.

13

The Weather

SINCE the last glaciation, the main agent acting upon the landscape of Britain has been that perpetual preoccupation of the British people, the weather. It has eroded the rocks and affected the distribution of plants, animals and people. It influences the look, character and even the hourly moods of the countryside.

Britain's much-maligned climate often gives rise to breathtaking cloudscapes such as these in northern Scotland (right) and the Isle of Anglesey (above)

Another Ice Age?
There is always much popular argument about whether or not Britain is about to enter a fifth Ice Age, and although the years since the 1950s have tended to be colder and wetter than during the previous century, this may only be one of many minor cycles in the weather. Summers can still be hot and dry, with thunderstorms in July and August and often a golden Indian Summer, as it is called, in autumn; winter even in Scotland may be mild, and springs are invariably fickle. Many country people have a wealth of weather lore, from 'red sky at night, shepherd's delight', to a belief in a hard winter following a good crop of hawthorn berries or an early departure of swallows. Few can be relied upon. Such particular and noticeable associations as hard winters and hawthorn berries relate rather to the previous winter than to the subsequent one.

Not that the British climate is extreme in any way. Over the centuries there have been sometimes prolonged shifts in temperature, like the cold, wet period which lasted from the middle of the 16th to the 19th centuries, but these have been more marked because on the whole Britain has a moderate and consistent pattern of weather. The highest temperature on official record is 36.7 degrees Centigrade, recorded at Epsom in August 1911, and the lowest was at Braemar both in 1895 and again on 10th January 1982, minus 27.2 degrees. Rain is plentiful and consistent throughout the year – it falls on more than 200 days on the western hills of Wales and Scotland – but rarely torrential. The particular characteristic of the British weather is actually its moderation: what makes it so eternally popular as a subject of conversation is its constantly changing and very localized pattern.

The influence of the sea
When Britain became an island about 7,000 years ago, it came under the influence of the 3,000 miles of Atlantic Ocean to the west. The prevailing winds were from the west, too, and areas of low barometric pressure called depressions or 'lows' began their endless movement eastward. Air from the regions of high pressure over the colder, dryer land masses of northern Europe and the Arctic was drawn in to these low pressure areas. The spirally blowing winds around the depressions, moving in a generally anti-clockwise direction and carrying the moist sea air with them, met the land barrier of the British Isles and so the air was forced to rise, to cool, and condense to form clouds and rain.

Another name for a depression or area of low pressure is a

cyclone – hence the more familiar use of the term 'anti-cyclone' for a system of high pressure in Britain's weather forecasts. Occasionally the winds around Britain can reach enormous force as an intense depression sucks in surrounding air. In 1808 Admiral Sir Francis Beaufort, Hydrographer to the Navy, devised the Beaufort Scale which now defines the force of winds. Force 0 is calm: smoke rises vertically and the sea is like a mirror. At Force 1 the wind speed is one to three miles an hour and smoke drifts. At Force 5, described as a 'fresh breeze', the wind speed has risen to around 20 miles an hour and white horses appear on the sea. At Force 8, a 'fresh gale', it is difficult to walk against the wind and whole trees may be in violent motion. At Force 12 the wind becomes a hurricane with speeds between 73 and 82 miles per hour.

Weaker depressions can lose the fight against high pressure areas or anti-cyclones which may build up over the Continent, and the British Isles are often the scene of busy encroachments and retreats of these different weather factions, so that there may be floods in the south-west and cloudless sunshine in the north-east, or as little as 50 miles or so between two entirely different kinds of weather. A cloudless day is actually quite uncommon in Britain, since a calm clear sky in the early morning often gathers cloud masses as warm pockets of air rise, cool, condense and become visible as droplets.

Clouds

Clouds are fascinating to watch. The highest are more than 18,000 feet up, formed of ice crystals, producing the feathery cirrus or mare's tails, and sometimes a milky veil of cirrostratus. At a lower level are the white masses of cumulus, perpetually changing, making swift shadows on the sunlit countryside below. Altocumulus is often seen in the evening, forming a 'mackerel sky', as delicately patterned as the mackerel's scales and often as luminously coloured pink and violet. Sometimes the frothy cumulus clouds tower into the icy air above, and assume the shape of a great towering anvil: these are cumulonimbus, or thunder-clouds, containing up to 50,000 tons of water and presaging heavy rain or hail. Grey, damp days usually mean low cloud, often moving in from the sea. These are either nimbostratus, which may cover the whole sky in a dull blanket, or the more broken stratocumulus. All stratus cloud is formed as a sheet, and more often than not it means rain.

Rain and the landscape
Rain has carved out much of the landscape of Britain, whether through its passage in streams and rivers or by its slow erosion beneath the surface. In granite upland areas with thin acid soils the rain runs swiftly away and adds little to what meagre nutriment is already there; in less impoverished soils it soaks through layers of

The stalactite chambers of Gough's Cave in Cheddar Gorge

permeable rocks until it lies on the impermeable levels below, making its way out in the form of springs at those points where the impermeable rocks appear on the surface.

In limestone areas rain can act as a weak acid, dissolving cracks and joints between massive subterranean chunks of stone. The caves at Cheddar Gorge and Wookey Hole in the Mendips of Somerset were formed by the gradual wearing away of such seams between the rocks, until roofs crashed and waterfalls cascaded in the darkness beneath the earth.

The Hand of Man

MODERN man is thought to have appeared in Europe some 40,000 years ago, and on the Continent there is considerable evidence of the art and culture of Palaeolithic *homo sapiens*. But in Britain there are few signs of forays by our early ancestors into what was then a grim Arctic region of a single land mass. Not until the first cold, damp centuries of the post-glacial period, about 8,300 years BC, did men cross the swamps of the North Sea and the wide valley of the English Channel into this bleak northern wilderness.

Nomadic man

The first men were hunters and fishermen, wildfowlers, gatherers of wild fruits, plants and fungi, as much a part of their environment as any other animal. They must have had a true culture of their own, based on a nomadic life in the forests; although they did not cultivate the land they probably cleared small areas for temporary settlement during the season of hunting or gathering autumn harvests, particularly as the climate became kindlier, with warmer, dryer summers and ever increasing woodland in Britain.

Yet even while nomadic wanderers were moving north to Britain, there were already farms and peaceful settlements in the Middle East, the emergence of great civilizations to come. From these distant lands other migrants were moving across Europe. No one knows how well they integrated, if at all, with the existing sparse population of Britain: the time scale is vast, and it is impossible to estimate whether they came as invading forces, or as small, independent groups simply seeking new lands to farm. For these were not hunters, at least not primarily, but cultivators and livestock farmers. They brought with them a new age: the New Stone Age, the time of Neolithic peoples. It began in about 5000 BC.

The New Stone Age

It is increasingly clear that the early Neolithic inhabitants of Britain made a considerable impression on the landscape. There was a heavy rainfall at this period, a warm and moist coastal climate that encouraged dense forests even in the more northern parts of Scotland, with oak and elm encroaching on the hardier Scots pine. Patches had to be cleared in these forests by felling and burning, sometimes only temporarily until the farmers moved on to new soils, or more permanently, as on the generous Wessex downlands, where marks of Neolithic settlement remain today. One of their great 'causewayed camps' survives on Windmill Hill in Wiltshire, which gives its name to this particular type of Neolithic culture. Enclosures like Windmill Hill were probably intended for keeping livestock safe rather than for defence.

It is easy to underestimate the practical and indeed technological powers of these early people, but it is now thought that they farmed very considerable areas of both southern and more northern England. They quarried flints in sophisticated mines like those at Grimes Graves in East Anglia, made pottery and all kinds of tools, and they were extraordinarily skilled builders. Within sight of Windmill Hill is the huge mound of Silbury Hill, so little eroded over the centuries that it remains massive – and mysterious – today. No one knows why it was built: it does not appear to be a burial mound, like the many great earth barrows in which mass graves have been discovered, or like the slightly later long barrows which were built of blocks of drystone walling.

Another monument to the people of late Neolithic times is the 'henge', a circular enclosure usually ramparted by a bank and ditch and set round with wood or stone pillars. One of the most impressive of all henge monuments, Avebury, covers 28 acres, and took untold millions of man-hours to build.

Kits Coty House, a Neolithic burial chamber near Aylesford in Kent. The stones that form the chamber were originally covered by a huge earthen mound

The Hand of Man

Oldbury Castle, an Iron Age hillfort near Yatesbury in Wiltshire. Forts such as this usually consist of a series of defensive banks and ditches, with entrances which were protected by further earthworks and wooden gates and sentry-walks

Roman advances

Agriculture expanded enormously in Roman times, with both domestic and export markets opened up for the first time. There were good roads, excellent communications, and new towns and outposts of Empire through which to trade. All kinds of mining and manufacture flourished. New imperial estates and prosperous villas were established in the secure lowlands. Skilled engineers began to drain the fens of East Anglia. Farming methods were not noticeably advanced, but millions of acres were under production. Timber was felled for charcoal burning and the smelting of iron: quarries were opened, salt mines developed and ports expanded. Hadrian's Wall made its serpentine way across the northern hills, as fine a feature of the landscape as has ever been designed.

Ages of bronze and iron

New immigrants from the Continent continued the development of the henges. The new arrivals were farmers, but they were also skilled in working with metals, particularly copper and tin, which produce the alloy bronze. They arrived in about 1,900 BC and brought with them the Bronze Age. The earliest settlers are known as the Beaker Folk, because of the characteristic beaker or small handleless mug often found in their graves with a variety of very beautiful metal objects.

Over succeeding centuries there was prosperity in Britain, with increasing forest clearance for arable and livestock farming. Some of our modern heathland goes back to such clearances. Villages were established, particularly in the south-west of England. Some later fortified hill settlements, however, suggest a need for defence, perhaps against raiding parties from other tribes. But in about 500 BC there was a new threat from the south and west: a rapidly increasing population in Europe was putting pressure on people to move northward to find new lands, new territories, and the first Celtic invaders forced the peaceful Bronze Age inhabitants of Britain to retreat into the uplands or build more defensive fortresses. Not that all were necessarily aggressive. The earliest migrants introduced new ploughing methods and settled on the sunny downland slopes.

It was the successive waves of Celtic invaders who brought with them war chariots, strange and bloody spiritual beliefs and a knowledge of iron. They came from France, the Rhineland and the Low Countries, and rapidly expanded the mining of metal ores as well as their agriculture. New kinds of settlement date from this Iron Age, like the stone broch towers

of Scotland and the resettled Bronze Age village of Jarlshof in Shetland and the crannogs, or raft-based hut villages which were built on artificial islands in the lakes and swamps around Glastonbury and Mere in Somerset. Most characteristic of all were the huge ramparted hillforts found throughout the western uplands of Britain.

The people of the Iron Age were widespread, clever and energetic. Long before Julius Caesar crossed the Channel in 55 and 54 BC there was considerable trade and political contact with Rome. The Belgae people of the south-east of England were one of the most powerful influences in the country, and it was their support of other expanding and aggressive tribes on the Continent that made Caesar seek to quell their ambitions.

Romans and Saxons

When the Romans finally occupied Britain in AD43 and turned it into a Roman province, they had an easier job than many of the Roman legionaries might have expected: it was not quite the barbaric wilderness they had believed. Yet there is no doubt that the dark Druid religion of the Celtic people had a decidedly unpleasant side. Violence flared up in AD 60 in a ferocious rebellion led by the widowed Queen Boudicca of the Iceni. The people marked their lives by the seasons, birth and death, the feasts of Beltane, Samain, and Lammas. Julius Caesar said of them that they measured time not in days, but in nights. For many people the rule of Rome was kinder than that of the Celtic chieftains. For some 400 years military and civilian administrations ran Britain, during which it was more consistently at peace than ever before – or indeed since. No wonder that in the dark times to follow old men remembered it as a Golden Age.

Following the departure of the Romans, the urban network which was the basis of life in Britain dwindled and died. Villas became isolated, self-sufficient homesteads. The invading Saxons and Danes, who filled the anarchic vacuum of Romanized Celtic peoples with their own essentially pastoral system of thegns, or lords, peasants and slaves, expanded this self-sufficient agricultural economy.

The Saxons favoured the lowland areas of Britain. They cleared great tracts of forest to cultivate open fields with heavy ploughs and teams of oxen, dividing them into communally cultivated strips about 200 yards long and ten to 20 yards wide. In upland areas the older Celtic system of small grazing fields, often enclosed, was continued.

Hadrian's Wall, the finest British monument to Roman engineering and endeavour. It originally stretched for about 73 miles from Bowness, on the Solway Firth, to Wallsend, near the mouth of the Tyne

Bronze Age builders

The people of the Bronze Age were great builders. Their unique monument is Stonehenge in Wiltshire. It was constructed over a period of several centuries, using massive sarsen stones from north Wiltshire and smaller but still huge boulders from the Preseli Mountains in Wales – the Blue Stones. At some time these stones were manoeuvred into great trilithons standing in a double circle – some of the lintel stones weigh as much as 50 tons, and they are not only tongued-and-grooved together but mortised and tenoned into the uprights. The uprights themselves are carved to eliminate the illusory tapering effect when seen from ground level – a concept usually believed to be Greek.

No one knows the reason for such extraordinary constructions – and stone circles occur in many parts of Britain, including the Highlands of Scotland and the Western Isles – but they do seem to have had astronomical associations. Their sophistication is extraordinary. Stonehenge was built with such knowledge and precise observation of the heavens that it must have had some profound significance. The men of the Wessex Bronze Age Culture who built it were warriors and traders: they sailed from the Baltic to the Mediterranean. One theory is that such a precise astronomical and indeed navigational instrument as Stonehenge was a part of a strong seafaring aristocracy.

The Hand of Man

By ancient right of pannage, established in medieval times, commoners may let their pigs roam free in the New Forest at times when the nut crop is considered to be sufficiently abundant

Norman forests

Forest still covered about one third of the country in Norman times, and there were ferocious penalties for poaching on the royal hunting grounds. Yet the common people did retain certain rights. They could graze cattle and sheep by the right of the common of pasture, take small branches of wood and brushwood by right of estovers, graze their pigs on acorns or beechmast by right of pannage or 'mast' as it was known in the New Forest; they could fish by right of piscary, and cut peat or turf for fuel by right of turbary. Peat cutting, indeed, was responsible for the lovely waterways of the Norfolk Broads. But this minor clearance and grazing was enough to constrict the regeneration of the forest lands. Small saplings could not survive it. And the Normans had introduced the rabbit, too, which did severe damage.

The Medieval countryside

The Norman invasion coincided with an expanding European economy. Agriculture did not change under the new rule, although it substituted feudal serfdom for churldom and slavery, and there were further expansions of farmland to meet the demand for produce both at home and abroad. Royal hunting forests were defined – the very word forest comes from the Latin phrase *forestem silvam*, meaning 'the wood outside' (that is, beyond the estates of castles, manors, churches and monasteries). With the Normans came the great pioneering monastic foundations of the Cistercians, who by 1170 had established about 40 monasteries in remote areas of the country. They specialized in wool: Melrose Abbey alone had about 12,000 breeding sheep, and the bare golden uplands of the Scottish borders were nibbled clear of oak trees.

Another, more organized destruction of woodland was the practice of assart, or the deliberate clearance of trees. It was allowed in parts of the royal forests – as long as the king was paid. In 1204 King John agreed to the deforestation of the whole of Devon except Exmoor and Dartmoor.

A dramatic rise in population took place between the 11th and the end of the 13th centuries, and there was increased pressure on the land as people cleared and colonized the most unlikely areas in their efforts to feed themselves. There were settlements even on the thin soils of Dartmoor, on the Yorkshire Dales and the Scottish Highlands. It was a process grimly reversed when the great plague killed some 40 per cent of the population between 1348 and 1349.

For more than a century the plague ravaged Britain. Many

villages were deserted during the 14th and 15th centuries and the first to be abandoned were those which had so desperately been established on the poorest land, like that at Hound Tor on Dartmoor of which traces still remain. The weather worsened, too, becoming colder and wetter. Harvests failed and livestock suffered. The economy was in bleak recession. Where woodland had been cleared, it began, over a number of years, to revert to rough heathland and scrub.

Industry and the loss of woodlands

Prosperity came again to Britain during the time of the Tudors and the Stuarts – a time when the population of the country virtually tripled. Trade, agriculture and especially industry all expanded, with accompanying prosperity for some and uneasy impoverishment for the many landless labourers who began to suffer through early enclosure of land and a lack of employment. Once again there was a land hunger, and a new pressure on the countryside from the 80 per cent of the population who lived and tried to work on the land.

But it was industry which was making real inroads into the still wooded and pastoral landscape. The blast furnace was introduced at the time of Queen Elizabeth I, and British iron was recognized as the best in the world: the iron and steel industries expanded enormously, as did charcoal-burning for smelting throughout the country. Lead, copper, tin and coal were all mined in quantity. Everything needed timber for fundamental fuel: ship and house-building, glass-making, milling, brewing, every process of craft and manufacture. Even the new hops of Kent demanded timber for poles and charcoal for the oast houses. Industry was moving out to its sources of fuel: ironworks were opened in the Forest of Arden, and consumed it too. Even the forests of the wealds of Sussex and Kent, famous for charcoal burning since before the Romans, began to run short of standing timber. In some districts even the cottagers went cold and hungry because there was simply no wood for fuel, and sea-coal, so called because it was transported by sea from the coalfields of north-eastern England began to be widely used. It was much disliked, and its yellow sulphurous smoke began to discolour many towns.

There were still forests, of course, wild places in the hills and the western uplands. But it was not easy to transport loads of timber over long distances. The roads were poor and horsepower put a physical limitation on transport.

An aerial photograph of Laxton, Nottinghamshire, where the open field system of farming, first introduced by the Saxons, is still practised

Planting trees

As early as 1580 there was concern about the lack of trees, particularly oaks, whose timber was important to the building of both houses and ships. In that year Lord Burleigh ordered acorns to be sown on 13 acres of Windsor Park, the first recorded instance of forest planting. With the Restoration of Charles II in 1660 there came a renewed interest in tree planting, and in 1662 John Evelyn, the diarist, was made a member of a committee whose specific task was to answer the problem of the shortage of oak trees for building His Majesty's warships. Evelyn made a swift but exhaustive study of Britain's trees, the results of which were published in his great work *Sylva*. A second edition was published in 1670, and in its dedication to Charles II, Evelyn claimed that his book had been the 'sole occasion of furnishing your almost exhausted Dominions with more than two millions of timber trees'.

It was the beginning of a uniquely British and at first almost entirely amateur enthusiasm for trees, which resulted in the paradox that although the country is now one of the least densely forested in Europe it has a greater richness and diversity of species than any other comparable area. There were great numbers of amateur arboriculturalists like Robert Slayner Holford, who began to plant a collection of trees at Westonbirt in Gloucestershire in 1829. Today it is world famous as Westonbirt Arboretum, one of the finest collections of trees anywhere.

21

Petworth Park, Sussex – a landscape created by Capability Brown in the middle of the 18th century. The house and grounds are now owned by the National Trust

Landowners and the landscape
As farming prospered in the 18th and 19th centuries, so did the landowners, and they began to look at the landscape with an aesthetic as well as a calculating eye. Tree planting and conscious design of parkland and estates became immensely fashionable. Foxhunting and shooting resulted in the cultivation of woodlands, spinneys as coverts for game. Much of what we now think of as old or even ancient woodland was planted about 200 years ago by people who confidently believed in the future – people like those depicted in Gainsborough's painting of Mr and Mrs Andrews. It is clear that the prospect of 200 years to come held no terrors for them. They pose in perfect youthful complacency, the minor landed gentry of England, with dog, gun and garden seat, set in the plump and golden Suffolk countryside of the 18th century.

An age of enclosures

Farming was to make many far-reaching changes to the landscape from the 18th century onwards. Enclosure of common land had been happening piecemeal for hundreds of years, according to the local opportunities, but between 1760 and 1830 it was accelerated by Acts of Parliament and increasing social and economic change in the countryside. The results were various, and not always immediately adverse for the small farmers, cottagers and traditional squatters who had always relied on access to common or waste lands for their livelihood: new work was created by the demands for fencing, hedging, new buildings and roads. Certainly they were almost always beneficial for landowners and the larger tenant farmers. There is no doubt that although enclosure was not wholly responsible for the patterns of hedges and drystone walls in the countryside, it was largely the cause of the patchwork of mixed livestock and arable farming which is only now reverting to a different kind of open field system.

The Industrial Revolution

The 18th and 19th centuries saw dramatic changes in the landscape. The Industrial Revolution shook the foundations of British society, made unprecedented demands on natural resources, and transformed the country's predominantly rural face into a land pocked with mills, mines and furnaces. Factories, workshops, rows of streets, whole towns, sprang up in areas previously remote from industrial pressures. The rural poor moved in their thousands into the new manufacturing centres, often exchanging rural poverty for urban squalor. Mass production brought factory-built wagons, tools, and

building materials into the countryside. Traditional craftsmen found that their skills were no longer required, and the countryside began to lose its most individual and idiosyncratic characteristics. There were, of course, many advantages in this new world. Mass production meant cheap goods, available to many; scientific advances led to improvements in medicine, food production, and innumerable other aspects of life. Improved communications, especially the advent of the railways, brought the population of Britain closer together than ever before. Regional differences, once so striking, began to disappear. Perhaps all these changes would have been more easily assimilated into the countryside had it not been for World War I – which forced recognition of changing ways and made further drastic change inevitable.

The 1930s saw a recession not only in the general economy but in land values. It would have been a good time to buy up land for conservation, but nobody thought of it then. There was a considerable conservation movement awakening in Britain, but it was concerned with preserving the remaining wild areas, mostly moor and mountain, for public access, rather than with the hitherto gradual developments in agriculture which had made no great changes to the look of the countryside for more than a century. When World War II came, it was too late.

Suddenly an efficient agriculture was top priority. Food was essential – and food produced in Britain. Acres of old meadow and hitherto unploughed downland went under the plough during the war. It was the beginning of perhaps the most subtle, yet most far-reaching and irrevocable change in the British countryside which had ever taken place. Modern science and technology began to replace traditional farming skills, which had never fundamentally interfered with the processes of nature. Farming has now become almost entirely mechanized: fertilizers have eliminated old rotations, and the very look of the landscape is changing to something paradoxically more akin to the open fields of medieval times.

One thing is certain. The land is never still. The mountains may look eternal, but even they are still eroding, weathering, moving. The British countryside, in all its diversity, is ever-changing, being impoverished in one part while enriched in another, the subject of endless controversy. Yet it is always fascinating, always a source of inspiration to poets, painters, musicians, and anyone who stops a car for a moment to look at the view, or stands on a hill to see it spread before him.

Old and new. One of Nottinghamshire's few remaining windmills, the early 19th-century tower mill at North Leverton, overlooked by the cooling towers of West Burton power station

Where now?
Since World War II the pace of change in the countryside has quickened to a headlong rush. Many still remember horse-drawn hay wagons, stooks at harvest time, and chickens feeding in the farmyard. Until the 1950s many cottages, even in the southern counties, had no electricity, no mains drainage, no bathroom and an outside privy. Barely 30 years later almost every cottage boasts an array of gadgets and appliances undreamt of in the days of mangles and flat irons.

Motorways have carved great slices across the countryside, new towns have spread like fungus over high quality farmland, reservoirs have drowned villages and valleys, nuclear power stations lurk like dark monsters among some of our wildest scenery. Each year more of Britain disappears under concrete or brick. Each year more woodland, wetland, meadowland, is felled, drained or ploughed. Conservationists fight every inch of the way, but even though the conservationist lobby is strong, as many battles are lost as are won. In less than a hundred years we have destroyed landscapes that had been shaped and moulded by nearly 10,000 years of man's activities – how much will be left at the end of the next century?

The Living Countryside

Ever charming, ever new,
When will the landskip tire the view!
The fountain's fall, the river's flow,
The woody vallies warm and low;
The windy summit, wild and high,
Roughly rushing on the sky!
The pleasant seat, the ruin'd tow'r,
The naked rock, the shady bow'r;
The town and village, dome and farm,
Each give each a double charm.......

from Grongar Hill by John Dyer 1701-57

The Meadows

MEADOWS and pastures, rich in wild flowers and grasses, are a traditional part of the British landscape. But in the last 50 years most ancient meadows have either been ploughed up or re-seeded with quick-growing grasses. However, meadows bright with flowers can still be found, and some that have never been ploughed or treated with modern chemicals are preserved in parts of the country, especially along the upper Thames valley and in parts of East Anglia.

When farms were virtually self-supporting, meadows and pastures were an essential part of the countryside scene. They provided hay for winter feed and were grazed by cattle and horses in the summer. In the years after World War II, arable farming became much more profitable and thousands of acres of meadowland disappeared.

Hay meadows

There are several different kinds of meadows and pastures; the types are partly dictated by the soil on which they are found and partly by the agricultural methods used on them in the past. The richest meadows, from a naturalist's point of view, are those on neutral (neither too acid or too alkaline) lowland soils which may never have been ploughed and are still managed in the traditional way. Such meadows are often flooded in wet winters. Many of these are hay meadows, cut in June or July. By early summer many of the flowers have finished flowering and have seeded, so no harm is done to them if they are mown. Cutting at this time also encourages a greater variety of plants by hindering the growth of more pernicious plants that would eventually crowd out the delicate flowers if they went on growing. Farmers often actively encouraged the early flowering plants because they added extra sweetness and nourishment to the hay. One of these is sweet vernal grass, which flowers early in the year and is the secret essence of meadows since it contains a substance called coumarin which lends a sweet smell to the hay.

Probably the most famous of all flowers of lowland meadows is the snakeshead fritillary. This lovely flower, in bloom in early May, is now restricted in its wild state to some 20 meadows in England, although at the beginning of the century it was found in 27 different counties.

The upland limestone meadows of the

Pennines are also rich in wild flowers, and have specialities of their own, such as the globeflower and wood cranesbill, that are not found in lowland meadows. Another flower confined to northern meadows is the exquisite, coral-pink, bird's eye primrose.

Fields yellow with buttercups are still a common sight. This is because buttercups contain a chemical that is poisonous to cattle and they will not eat them. However, the poison disappears once they have been cut and dried, and the buttercups can then be safely eaten with the rest of the hay crop.

Wet meadows

Water meadows were once widespread throughout southern England, but are now rarely seen. These meadows were deliberately flooded each winter by an elaborate arrangement of channels, ditches and sluices. Flooding the meadows in this way encouraged an early flush of grass in the spring, providing grazing much earlier than on grass that had been exposed to low temperatures all winter.

The Washlands of East Anglia, found principally along the River Ouse, are meadows which are inundated by floodwater from surrounding fields in winter. Thousands of wading birds can often be seen in these meadows in winter, and in summer they provide an ideal habitat for rarer waders and several kinds of duck.

Key

1 Lapwings
2 Meadow buttercup (*May–July*)
3 Timothy grass
4 Yellow rattle (*May–September*)
5 Mole
6 Mole hill
7 Red clover (*May–October*)
8 Mole hills
9 Meadow fescue
10 Yorkshire fog
11 Common green grasshopper (*adults active late June–October*)
12 Dandelion (*March–October*)
13 Meadow brown butterfly (*on wing June–September*)
14 Common bumble bee
15 Field vole
16 Meadow foxtail
17 Cowslip (*April–May*)
18 Perennial rye grass
19 Lapwing on nest
20 Early purple orchid (*April–June*)
21 Dung
22 Meadow grasshopper (*adults active late June–November*)
23 Dung flies
24 Dung beetle
25 Daddy long legs (*crane fly; on wing summer and autumn*)
26 Milk maids (*also known as lady's smock or cuckoo flower; April–June*)
27 Short-tailed vole
28 Crested dog's-tail
29 Water avens (*May–August*)
30 Orange tip butterfly (*on wing May–June*)
31 Swallow (*summer visitor*)
32 Little owl
33 Meadow-sweet (*June–September*)
34 Cinnabar moth (*on wing May–June*)
35 Horse tail
36 Water forget-me-not (*May–September*)
37 Common soft rush
38 Swallow (*summer visitor*)
The animals and plants are not drawn to scale. Plants are in flower during the months shown in brackets

The Wetlands

Fens and marshes

FENS are areas of low-lying, waterlogged ground where decayed plant remains have accumulated over thousands of years to form peat. Unlike acid peat bogs, fen peat contains lime and is therefore alkaline. This makes it attractive to a large number of different plant species.

Marshes are more widespread and develop on inorganic deposits – often silts washed down rivers. They are usually found in low-lying valleys and beside lakes and large ponds.

Marshland and flooded meadows along the River Test near Stockbridge in Hampshire. Willows, among the first trees to colonize wetland sites, have grown up on drier areas among the reeds

Swallowtail butterfly
This lovely insect is found only in the Norfolk Broads, though attempts have been made to establish it in the Cambridgeshire fens. It was once widespread in British wetlands, but as these disappeared so did the milk parsley which is the only plant the swallowtail caterpillars eat. Adult swallowtails are on the wing in May and June.

Fens

The largest remaining areas of undrained fenland in Britain are in East Anglia, although scattered fenland remnants occur in other parts of the country. East Anglia's fenland once covered a vast area of low land that was filled with deep layers of peat, and, in some areas, silts. Although the Romans – realizing that under the fenland waters there were very rich soils – drained some areas, drainage on a large scale was not begun until the 17th century. Up until that time the Fens had been a land apart, virtually inaccessible and with a fiercely independent population who had their homes on the islands of clay and gravel which rose from the surrounding watery wilderness. The advantages of living in these strange waterlogged lands were many; not the least of them being that the outside world was kept well away. So when the drainage schemes were begun – mainly by the Duke of Cumberland and his Dutch engineer Cornelius Vermuyden – the fen people objected; at first in the courts, but when legal methods failed, by rioting. These rioters became known as the 'Fen Tigers'.

Today's drained fens are some of the richest and most fertile farmlands in the world. They have two extraordinary features – their complete flatness, with not a hillock for mile after mile, and the arrow-straight rivers and drainage channels or 'drains'. A few areas of undrained fenland are left, and nearly all of these are nature reserves. The most famous is Wicken

Left: a reed-fringed channel in Wicken Fen, a National Trust nature reserve near Ely in Cambridgeshire. It is one of the few undrained fenland sites remaining in East Anglia and supports a wide variety of birds, insects and plants – some of them extremely rare

Fen, Cambridgeshire, which displays the unique characteristics of fenland.

One of the most striking things about it is that it is many feet above the surrounding farmlands. This is because the peat in the farmlands shrank and decomposed as it was drained, leaving Wicken Fen as a raised island of wet peat. The fenland reserves are kept wet by a complex series of pumps and channels bringing water from surrounding land; even so drying-out is a continual problem, and scrub and trees are tending to invade the reed beds. This natural succession is kept in check by clearing the scrub and also by creating new stretches of open water. On some of the fens reeds are still cut regularly for thatching, and this also helps to preserve the open, wet conditions. Some of the fenlands that once covered the Somerset Levels survive, though these too are threatened by drainage and grass-improvement schemes.

The Broads

Found principally along the rivers Waveney, Yare and Bure and their tributaries, the Broads are some of the most unusual stretches of open water in Britain. It used to be thought that they were natural lakes occurring as part of the silting-up process of estuaries, but it has been known since the 1950s that they are peat-diggings created between the 11th and 13th centuries which were subsequently flooded when the sea level rose by a number of inches.

Several factors threaten the existence of the Broads today, and only determined efforts can save them. Many are shrinking in size as natural succession from marsh to scrub then woodland takes place. Pollution caused by run-off of chemicals and fertilizers from surrounding farmland threatens the delicate wildlife balance, and the tremendous popularity of the Broads as a holiday area is also damaging this fascinating wetland area.

Marshes

Still widespread in many parts of the country, marshes and wetlands are nonetheless threatened by reclamation for arable use, and by land drainage which is constantly lowering the water table. Where marshes remain they provide habitats for an exceptionally large number of plants and animals.

An important plant of wetlands is the common reed, which may form extensive beds. It can grow in a variety of conditions – from fairly deep water to almost dry land. In winter the reed dies right back, leaving corn-coloured stalks among which the new young shoots appear in spring. Reed beds make ideal habitats for nesting birds, particularly warblers like the sedge, reed and grasshopper warblers. Another common bird of reed beds is the reed bunting. Roe deer sometimes lay up in reed beds all day, emerging periodically to feed on the surrounding land. Insects spend the winter months protected from the cold inside the hollow stems of the dead reeds.

Marshes are in a process of continual change. Where rivers are slow-flowing, silts accumulate and plants take root. As more and more plants colonize a marshy area, so more and more dead vegetable matter accumulates. Eventually moisture-loving trees like alder and willow will be able to establish themselves on what was once open water.

Warblers of wetlands

Three warblers are commonly associated with wetland areas. The sedge warbler is present in Britain from April to September, and, as its name implies, it likes wet places and reed beds, but it can also be found in dense conifer plantations. Reed warblers live in the same places as sedge warblers, and the two species are often confused. Perhaps the easiest way to tell them apart is by their songs; the reed warbler has a continuous churring note, whereas the sedge warbler's churrs are interspersed by mimicry of the songs of other birds. Grasshopper warblers are often present in reed beds and thick undergrowth. Although they are difficult to see, their song is unmistakable; it has been likened to the sound made by a fishing line as it is reeled in. (Sedge and reed warblers are illustrated on pages 56–57.)

Snipe

Two species of snipe, common and jack, are found in Britain; but the much larger common can be seen all year round while the jack snipe is usually only a winter visitor. The common snipe is found in wetland habitats of all sorts, and its exceptionally long bill and striped plumage distinguish it from all other waders. In early spring, as part of the courtship display, snipe perform spectacular 'drumming' flights over their territories. The snipe dives out of the sky, twisting and turning as it does so, while the air passing through its outstretched outer tail feathers causes a vibrant, unearthly sound which carries for considerable distances.

Bittern

This shy bird, which spends most of its life hidden deep in reed beds and marshes, is increasingly rare through destruction of its habitat. If disturbed it will either 'freeze' with head pointing straight upwards, or flap clumsily away on wide and heavy wings. It is best appreciated when undisturbed and unseen, for then it may call from the dense vegetation in a deep, booming single note that can be heard up to a mile away. Bitterns breed mostly in East Anglia, but there are records of nests in other scattered localities. They can be seen in other parts of the country when on passage to Ireland, where they are regular winter visitors.

Heaths

EATHS have poor soil and therefore support only a limited number of plants and animals, but these habitats are of great interest because the plants and animals that do live in them are often especially adapted to the conditions, and because heaths can only be preserved by the direct intervention of man and his grazing animals.

Men control the future of heathlands, and it was men who created them in the first place. They were cleared of their natural vegetation during the Neolithic period – that is about 4,000 years ago. When more fertile soils became available for cultivation the heaths ceased to be needed for growing crops and they became grazing areas for cattle, sheep and goats. Overgrazing destroyed much good herbage and the poor soils were then colonized by plants like heather and gorse which can withstand both acid conditions and constant grazing.

Heathland management

Without grazing, or management by man, heaths would slowly revert to woodland. The trees most likely to colonize these areas are birches and pines, and both of these often form small groups on heathland. Traditionally, heaths are managed by carefully controlled burning. This kills seedling trees and other unwanted plants, but only destroys the dead growth and above ground parts of plants like heather. New shoots quickly grow from the undamaged roots, and the animals have fresh green growth to eat. However, if the fires are too hot, the underground parts of the plants, and even the exceptionally resilient seeds, will be killed.

Earthworms do not favour acid soil, so are not present in any numbers on heaths. Much of their work of breaking down plant material and aerating the soil is done in these conditions by ants. But ants cannot break down all the dead plant material that accumulates. This burns at very high temperatures if it is present in large quantities – another reason for controlled burning at regular intervals.

Heathland areas

Most of Britain's remaining heaths are confined to southern England, but there are some in the Midlands, and there are one or two heathland sites in northern England and Scotland. The New Forest has many acres of heath, and some of the finest heaths are found around Bournemouth and Swanage.

Surrey was once largely covered in heaths, and many of those which remain are now cared for by the National Trust. The Lizard Peninsula in Cornwall has extremely interesting areas of heathland which support plants and animals found nowhere else in Britain.

Breckland

East Anglia's Breckland is a unique kind of dry heathland habitat. Like other heaths it was created by early man, but its different soil structure means that it supports a flora found nowhere else.

Much of the soil here is sandy, and in some places extensive sand dunes can be seen. Many of these have now been stabilized by heathland plants and grasses, or by plantations of conifers, but in medieval times tremendous sand blows, which inundated whole villages, were not uncommon.

Many of the Breckland heaths became rabbit warrens in the Middle Ages, and it was rabbit-grazing that preserved the open character of much of the area. Myxomatosis has decimated the rabbit population, but today the parts of Breckland which remain are more threatened by the demands of modern agriculture.

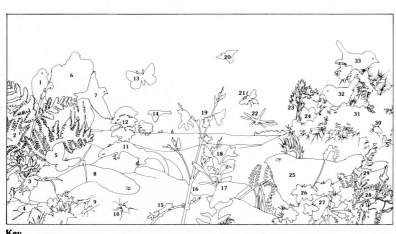

22 Golden ringed dragonfly (*on wing June–September*)
23 Sheep's fescue
24 Silver-studded blue butterfly (*on wing June–August*)
25 Nightjar (*summer visitor*)
26 Bell heather (*June–September*)
27 Fox moth (*on wing May–June*)
28 Dodder (*July–October*)
29 Ling (*July–September*)
30 Gorse shield bug
31 Gorse
32 Stonechat (*female*)
33 Stonechat (*male*)
The plants and animals are not drawn to scale. Plants are in flower during the months shown in brackets

Key

1 Linnet (*female*)
2 Bracken
3 Tormentil (*May–September*)
4 Tiger beetle (*adults active spring–summer*)
5 Grayling butterfly (*on wing July–September*)
6 Silver birch
7 Linnet (*male*)
8 Adder
9 Robber ants
10 Heath assassin bug (*adults active July–October*)
11 Common lizard
12 Scots pine
13 Common heath moth (*on wing May–August*)
14 Yellowhammer
15 Mottled grasshopper (*adults active June-October*)
16 Broom (*April–June*)
17 Emperor moth (*on wing April–May*)
18 Heath milk wort (*May–August*)
19 Broom (*April–June*)
20 Woodlark
21 Potter wasp

31

Moorland

OFTEN silent except for wind soughing through the vegetation, the occasional twitter of a meadow pipit, or liquid bubble of curlews in spring, moorlands are wild and lonely places which seem far removed from the influence of man.

But moorlands, like most of the rest of Britain's countryside, were created, in part at least, by men. Even today many heather moorlands are carefully managed so that they will support large numbers of grouse.

Red grouse

Thousands of acres of heather moorland, especially in northern England and Scotland, are carefully managed to encourage red grouse. Adult grouse eat almost nothing but heather, and they have become so well adapted to the moorland habitat that they cannot survive in other conditions. Grouse usually remain on the moors even in the most extreme weather conditions, though they occasionally leave very exposed sites to feed in lower fields. Young grouse need more protein than adults, and so a large part of their diet consists of invertebrates found living deep in the heather. In order to sustain large numbers of grouse for sporting purposes, heather moors are burned off in patches. This encourages the growth of succulent young heather shoots and a constant 'rotation' of heather of different ages for food, cover and nesting habitat.

There are many similarities between moorlands and heaths; both were once covered by forests, both occur on acid soils, and both were largely cleared of their natural tree cover by man. The clearing took place in many areas just at a time when the climate was becoming cooler and wetter, so that on the uplands where moorlands are found the denuded slopes became waterlogged and mosses began to grow. The most common of these were sphagnum mosses, which do not decay when they die, but slowly build up in layers of dead material that eventually become peat. Higher rainfall leached more and more minerals out of the already poor soils. The minerals, particularly iron, frequently formed a hard pan below the leached level, causing further waterlogging and thus encouraging further peat growth.

In the higher upland areas, particularly Scotland, north Wales and the Pennines, forest clearance probably only began on a large scale in medieval times. Scotland retained much of its tree cover until the 18th century, when demand for timber, clearances to increase sheep-grazing areas, and, in the 19th century, the great popularity of grouse-shooting and deer-stalking on open moors, created the moorland scenery that exists today.

In especially wet areas blanket bogs had already developed naturally and swamped the forests. Sphagnum is usually the dominant plant on such bogs, but sedges, including cotton grass, which has a white seed head like a ball of cotton wool, are abundant, and insectivorous plants are sometimes found. These plants, of which sundews are the commonest, obtain the nutrients they need to survive by trapping insects in their sticky leaves and ingesting the succulent juices. Bilberry sometimes becomes the dominant plant on shallower peat; it is usually found on higher slopes or in shaded woodlands.

Heather grows on dry peat and acid soils and is the most common plant on all drier moors. With the heather may be found bilberry, crowberry, purple moor grass, heath rush and

bracken. Bracken, which spreads vigorously by means of underground stems, is found throughout the country and it has been estimated that as much as 10% of our uplands are covered by it. It is extremely poisonous to cattle and horses, and its unchecked spread across the uplands is a cause of considerable anxiety to hill farmers.

Wildlife on the moors

Great numbers of invertebrates live deep in the damp moorland vegetation. These tiny creatures attract insect-eating birds, but since the insect population declines in winter and moorland winters can be very severe, many of these birds are only present in spring and summer. Waders, including curlews, golden plovers and dunlins, breed on the moors, but spend the winter months on the coast or fly to warmer climates. Meadow pipits are found in all upland areas, and twites – small finches – can be found on the moors of northern England. Another small bird which may be seen is the wheatear. Birds of prey include kestrels, sometimes merlins, and, in very restricted localities, red kites, hen harriers and golden eagles. Carrion crows and hooded crows find food in the form of other birds' eggs, insects and dead sheep. Mammals, except for sheep, are few and far between on moors as a rule; the most common are voles, which form a large part of the diet of the birds of prey and of upland foxes.

Red deer
Largest and most magnificent of our native mammals, the red deer was once widespread throughout Britain, but is now confined to upland and some well-wooded areas. The largest populations live in the Highlands of Scotland, where there may be as many as a quarter of a million, but smaller herds can be seen in the Lake District, the New Forest and on Exmoor. Herds are also often found confined in deer parks, with 'escapes' colonizing surrounding woodland.

Red deer live in groups, the males separate from the females and young for most of the year. During the mating season, in September and October, the stags compete with each other for a group of hinds. Sometimes the stags clash antlers in pitched battles, but disputes are often settled by prolonged roaring matches. In Scotland the deer spend the summer months high in the mountains, probably to get away from flies, and descend to the lower slopes in winter.

Downlands

T IS CHALK which gives downs their particular appearance and determines their special wildlife communities. But although chalk sweeps in a wide band from the Dorset coast up through East Anglia into the wolds of Yorkshire, and across from Wiltshire into Sussex along the North and South Downs, it is only in the southern counties that typical downland scenery is found on a large scale. This is because much of the chalk further north is covered by other material laid down in later geological periods, whereas in the south the chalk is on, or just under, the surface.

Man on the downs

Forests once covered the chalklands, but because the soil was shallow it was easily cleared, and the downs were among the first areas of Britain to be cultivated by man. At first he grew crops on them, but as the thin soils became exhausted, and as ploughs, which could turn over heavier soils, were introduced, the chalklands became pasture for grazing animals. It is the combination of soil type with grazing that has created the downland landscapes we know today. The grazing animals, principally sheep and, later, rabbits, kept the turf short and prevented the downs from reverting to scrub, then forest, by eating any seedling shrubs or trees that appeared. Lack of water also contributes to the unique flora of the downs. Chalk is an exceptionally porous material, so downs are usually very dry, encouraging some plants and discouraging others.

Downland which has not been ploughed for very long periods is exceptionally rich in plant life, and a square yard may contain as many as 40 different kinds of flowering plants. This habitat is now rapidly disappearing as more and more downland is either ploughed up or sprayed to encourage certain grasses. Today only about 3% of Britain's chalklands are covered by grass, and much of this has been radically altered by changing agricultural methods.

Animals and birds

Mammals and birds are not found in great numbers on open downland, but hares and rabbits are common, and in the past, when they swarmed in vast numbers, rabbits contributed immensely to the preservation of the downs. In high summer, skylarks may be the only birds seen on a downland walk, but sparrows, meadow pipits and wheatears are also often present. Kestrels find the open country ideal for hunting insects and small mammals like voles and mice, and they frequently nest in the isolated clumps of trees that dot the downs.

The downs today

The largest areas of unploughed downland to be found today are in Wiltshire, where thousands of acres are used as military training grounds. Most of the rolling chalk hills of the North and South Downs are once more under crops after a break of perhaps 4,000 years, but places can still be found where the typical downland flora flourishes. Some of the most important sites are now nature reserves.

Hillforts and other prehistoric earthworks can be rich hunting grounds for downland plants and insects. The kinds of flora found in such places will vary from the dry top of the banks to the wetter bottoms of the ditches. Ancient trackways, drove roads and green lanes cross the downs in great numbers and plants and animals which may have disappeared from the fields will be found along their verges. Chalkpits and quarries may also act as unofficial nature reserves.

Key

1 Marble white butterfly (*on wing July–August*)
2 Common quaking grass
3 Yellow rattle (*May–September*)
4 Large skipper (*on wing June–August*)
5 Striped snail
6 Round mouthed snail
7 Goatsbeard (*also known as jack-go-to-bed-at-noon; May–August*)
8 Meadow oat grass
9 Common blue butterfly (*on wing May–September*)
10 Harebell (*July–October*)
11 Wild marjoram (*July–September*)
12 Common field grasshopper (*adults active late June–November*)
13 Shepherd's crown (*a fossil sea urchin*)
14 Upright brome
15 Beech hanger
16 Meadow brown butterfly (*on wing June–September*)
17 Greater knapweed (*June–September*)
18 Flint nodules
19 Wrinkled snail
20 Pyramidal orchid (*June–August*)
21 Earthworks of hillfort
22 Sheep
23 Common spotted orchid (*May–August*)
24 Wild thyme (*June–September*)
25 Stemless thistle (*May–September*)
26 Kestrel
27 Ox-eye daisy (*May–September*)
28 Hare
29 Burnet moth (*on wing June–August*)
30 Hare
31 Field scabious (*June–October*)
32 Skylarks
The plants and animals are not drawn to scale. Plants are in flower during the months shown in brackets

The Hills

SOFTER and more gentle than mountains, the hills of Britain are as varied in the pleasures they afford as in the underlying rocks which give them shape. As physical elements of the landscape they lend a vital perspective to the countryside and act as backcloths to many of Britain's most beautiful areas. A selection of the most interesting hills is given on these pages.

The Wrekin is one of the most distinctive of Shropshire's hills, and has a special place in the hearts of many Salopians

The Chilterns
Part of the band of chalk that stretches from the Dorset coast across to East Anglia, the Chilterns are famous for their beechwoods and their rolling downlands. The hills rise from the Thames valley at Goring and run in a long arc to the rounded downlands above Dunstable and Luton. Although their highest point is less than 900 feet above sea level, the hills form a definite barrier between London's outer suburbs and the broad plains of central England. They rise gently beyond the capital, but the escarpment is impressively steep and has splendid viewpoints like Coombe Hill, near Princes Risborough, and Beacon Hill, above Wendover. There is a nature trail through downland on Beacon Hill, while fine beechwoods and lime-loving plants can be seen in the National Trust nature reserve off the A40 at Aston Rowant. Magnificent pollarded beeches and other ancient trees can be seen in Burnham Beeches, three miles north of Slough.

The Mendips
Grey limestone crags, dry gorges, bare uplands and marching drystone walls typify the scenery of the Mendips, which rise abruptly from the Somerset plain. They begin at Frome and extend westwards to Weston-super-Mare. Although the bulk of the Mendips is limestone, the highest points – Beacon Hill, Pen Hill and North Hill – are of old red sandstone that have weathered better than the rocks that surround them. On the north-western edge of the Mendips is Cheddar Gorge, a huge dry valley with towering limestone cliffs on either side. Here a tremendous variety of lime-loving plants – some of them rare – can be found, while on the plateau at the top large ant hills indicate the presence of ancient pasture. Ebbor Gorge, near Wookey Hole, is a National Trust nature reserve with fine valley woodlands composed mainly of ash.

The Cotswolds
Shaped like a huge wedge, the Cotswolds rise from the flat plains of Oxfordshire and culminate in a long escarpment that overlooks the vales of Evesham, Gloucester and Berkeley. A finger of Cotswold stone stretches southwards almost as far as Bath. The Cotswolds are given their remarkable unity by the oolitic limestones of which they are composed and from which most of their towns and villages are built. There are a great many sites of interest to the naturalist, and a large number of these can be found on the western escarpment. One of the best known is Crickley Hill, near Birdlip. River valleys like the Windrush, Coln and Churn are rich in flowers of marsh and meadow, especially in certain orchids. Walkers can follow the Cotswold Way, a 100-mile route that crosses the finest scenery between Chipping Campden and Bath.

A magnificent Iron Age fort crowns Herefordshire Beacon, one of the summits of the Malvern Hills, which rise to the south-west of Worcester

Ring Ouzel
Found on wilder and higher hills, the ring ouzel is a close relative of the blackbird. The two species are very similar in appearance, except that the ring ouzel has a white crescent on its chest. They are not easy birds to approach, being inclined to fly away through the undergrowth, but males can sometimes be seen singing from rocky perches.

Ancient pollarded beeches
Beech trees and woods
Considered by some to be Britain's most beautiful tree, the beech may live for up to 200 years and grow to nearly 150 feet. Its timber has long been valued for furniture-making, and beech is still grown for that purpose in the Chilterns.

Beech trees throw such dense shade that when they are in full leaf the floor of a beechwood may be almost without flowering plants, which demand sunlight. However, some plants thrive in the shade; these include many types of fungi, and some of our most unusual orchids. Invertebrates abound in the deep litter and dead wood that accumulates on the floor of a beechwood. These include beetles, spiders, earwigs and snails. The wealth of insects attracts some small mammals, and often badgers, while voles and mice eat beechmast and other plant material.

Shropshire Hills

Set between the River Severn and the Welsh border, the Shropshire hills are shaped like the fingers of a giant hand. Titterstone Clee reaches 1,750 feet above the Ludlow-Kidderminster road and looks northwards to 1,772-foot Brown Clee, Shropshire's highest point. The limestone ridge of Wenlock Edge is flanked by Corve Dale and Ape Dale, while Caer Caradoc, the Lawley and others stand above the village of Cardington. Near Church Stretton are the heather-clad sandstone slopes of the Long Mynd, and close to the Welsh border are the rocky summits of the Stiperstones and tree-clad Corndon Hill. Beyond the Severn rises an isolated hill that serves as a landmark for many miles around. This is the Wrekin, a huge whaleback of volcanic rock that rises to 1,334 feet. Of the hundreds of walks that can be taken in this fascinating area, one of the easiest follows Cardingmill valley (on the outskirts of Church Stretton) up on to the grouse moors of the Long Mynd. Dippers, wagtails, ring ouzels and grouse can all be seen within minutes of each other in this area.

The Cheviots

The Cheviots are a great dome of granite and other volcanic rocks that lie on the border between England and Scotland. The finest parts on the English side of the border are incorporated in the Northumberland National Park. Millions of years of weathering, and the smoothing action of glaciers, have left the Cheviots without any dramatic summits, yet the rolling expanses of heather and peat moorland provide some of the wildest and least-known hill scenery in Britain. One of the best ways to explore these hills is along unclassified roads from Rothbury (on the eastern border of the national park) up the valley of the River Coquet. The winding lanes make their way through splendid upland woods and eventually emerge in bare, windswept scenery far from the nearest village. From this point walkers can reach the series of Roman camps at Coquet Head, or follow the Pennine Way northwards along the English–Scottish border.

Forests, Woods and Trees

A damp clearing in the New Forest, with alders in the background. In the foreground is bog myrtle, an aromatic shrub that was once used to flavour beer

Woodland birds in winter
One of the best times of the year to see woodland birds is winter, when there are no leaves to interrupt the view. At this time members of the tit family and several other species flock together and travel from tree to tree exploring every nook and cranny for insects. Long-tailed tits, probably first noticed by their *zee-zee* calls, tend to travel in small family groups. These tiny birds are easily distinguished by their long tails and almost round bodies. Great tits, blue tits and sometimes marsh tits all flock together. Often found with these groups are nuthatches and treecreepers. Goldcrests are frequently present as well, but they are more likely to be seen in woods where there are evergreen trees.

Long-tailed tits are among the smallest British birds

Many other birds that in summer are more often associated with open fields and hedgerows take advantage of the additional protection and food possibilities of the woodlands in winter. Large flocks of chaffinches are likely to be seen feeding in fields at the edge of woodland, while bullfinches spend a good deal of time in the treetops. Also fond of the treetops are fieldfares, winter visitors from northern Europe, who feed in the open fields but fly into the trees with clattering calls if alarmed.

BRITAIN was clothed in thick forests for thousands of years after the last great ice sheets retreated. It used to be thought that the moors, heaths and mountainous regions of the country had survived much as they existed since the earliest times, but it is now known that the tree line stretched up to 3,000 feet, covering all but the highest and most barren peaks.

Nearly all of the denudation of the forests can be accredited to the hand of man, but climatic changes had a part to play. It is thought, for example, that a cooling of the climate at about the time of the early Iron Age prevented the natural regeneration of woodland cover in those areas already cleared by man. Conversely, the loss of tree cover may well have affected the climate and hastened the cooling process.

Today, only about 9% of Britain is covered by woodland; of this total about a quarter is deciduous woodland, the rest being coniferous forest largely created since the founding of the Forestry Commission in 1919.

Types of woodland
Although oak is the dominant tree in many British woods, other trees may also dominate a woodland scene.

Where the soil is waterlogged, discouraging most trees, alder woods tend to grow up. Many flooded valley bottoms must once have been covered in alder woods – or 'carrs' as they are known – but drainage and clearance have reduced these to scattered localities. Alder carrs can still be found in Norfolk, northern England and parts of Scotland.

Ash likes to grow in light, lime-rich soil, and for this reason ash woods are likely to have an extremely rich ground flora. Marvellous ash woods can be found in Yorkshire, Derbyshire, parts of Wales and in the West Country. In those areas ash may be the dominant tree, but in the south of the country it is usually found in woods that will eventually be dominated by beech trees. Beech only occurs naturally in the warmer climate of southern Britain, but has been widely planted throughout the country.

Below: An elderflower cluster

Most woods, however, have a mixture of trees in them. In oak woods, for example, there may be elm, sycamore, sweet chestnut, hornbeam, willow, wild cherry, and perhaps a dozen kinds of shrub. In the western half of the country woods of stunted oaks can be found cloaking isolated valley slopes. It was once thought that these woods were untouched survivors of prehistoric woodland, but it is now known that even these seemingly remote and wild woods were in fact altered and changed by men, who used their bark to tan leather. The plant life in these exposed western woods is usually very different from that in a lowland oakwood. Wild flowers may be few and far between, but a host of mosses, lichens and ferns may carpet the rocky floor and even grow on the trees themselves.

Woods then and now
Men have exploited woodland throughout history. Even the great royal forests, which are so often thought of as being examples of wild forest, were extensively managed and maintained, not only for the game that lived in them, but also for the trees themselves. At one time nearly a third of Britain was controlled by the Forest Law introduced by the Norman kings. Only a tiny remnant of these royal forests survives, but a careful study of them will show the great variety of uses to which they were put. Even today, when most woods appear neglected, many are in fact kept as cover for game or foxes. Some woods are still managed in traditional ways, especially in areas where furniture or fencing trades are important.

Jew's ear fungus

A Lowland Oakwood

THE ILLUSTRATION shows a lowland oakwood in early summer. If Britain's countryside were allowed to revert to forest, oaks would eventually be the dominant tree across most of the country. Two kinds of oak are native to Britain – pedunculate, which tends to prefer neutral soils, and sessile, which is often found on acid soil. (Pedunculate has acorns with stalks, or pedicles, and leaves growing straight from the twig. Sessile has leaves with stems and acorns without stems.) The two are often found growing together in the same wood, and hybrids are not uncommon.

Oaks support a greater variety of insect life than any other British tree, and as many as 280 different species have been counted on one tree. Of Britain's other native trees, the richest in insect life are willow, birch and hawthorn.

Of the plants in the illustration, ramsons is common in damp and shady places throughout Britain, while Solomon's seal is common only in southern counties. Early purple orchids can be found in woods and meadows throughout the country, and are usually easily identified since they are one of the first orchids to bloom; however, they vary in colour from almost pure white to deep purple and this can occasionally lead to confusion. Dog's mercury is one of the most common woodland plants, and often forms thick carpets.

41

Ancient Woodlands

Pollarded trees like these hornbeams in Epping Forest can still be seen in many royal forests and old deer parks

Early morning in the woods
Very early morning is one of the most exciting times to visit woodland. Badgers and foxes may be returning to their setts and earths; deer may be feeding in clearings, and the dawn chorous will be in full voice.

The dawn chorus starts about an hour before dawn in early summer, and it is generally the insect- and invertebrate-eating birds that are the earliest risers. Blackbirds and song thrushes are usually the first to sing, followed by crows and the grain-eating wood pigeon. Next come robins, pheasants, warblers and wrens.

Insects may also be heard above the bird song. Wasps can sound surprisingly loud as they chew through dead wood and plant stems collecting material for their nests, and hoverflies supply a constant background buzzing as they hang on invisible wings in shafts of morning sunlight among the leaves.

To WALK in Britain's mixed deciduous woods is not only to explore some of our richest wildlife habitats; it is also likely to be a journey through time – for many woods have histories that can be proved to stretch back to medieval times, and sometimes even further.

Although Britain is one of the most sparsely wooded countries in Europe, and although the loss of woodland throughout the country continues at a worrying rate, there are still thousands of acres of woods scattered across the country. Many of these are extremely ancient, and some, which the experts call primary woodlands, stand on sites that have been continuously wooded since prehistoric times. However, there are no survivors in Britain of the great primeval forests that once clothed most of the country; all of our woodlands have been more or less adapted and altered by man.

Living history
It is the primary woodlands which support the most varied and interesting kinds of wildlife. Indeed, one of the ways of identifying these ancient woods is by the flowers and plants which grow in them, for many wild plants spread very slowly and find it difficult to colonize new areas. Even such common woodland flowers as the bluebell, dog's mercury, and the wood anemone may indicate very ancient woodland, but there is no general rule of thumb that can be applied to ancient woods; only a very careful study of a wood's plants, its position and its recorded history is likely to prove its ancestry.

Woodland management

Nearly all British woodlands were managed, in one form or another, until 50 or 60 years ago. Managed woods, especially those with a mixture of tree species, provide a widely varied number of habitats for both flora and fauna.

The most common form of woodland management was coppice-with-standard, where large trees (standards) were allowed to grow to a considerable height over a period of perhaps a hundred years. Between the scattered standard trees were coppiced trees and shrubs, most often hazel, sycamore or chestnut, which were cut in blocks on a rotational basis. This form of management created a variety of habitats in each wood. In the areas recently cut back, wild flowers flourished, and in the areas becoming well-grown, birds could find nesting sites and food. One of the many side-effects of woodland management was that coppicing (cutting back growth to ground level) and pollarding (cutting back growth above the height of grazing animals so that they could not damage the new shoots) prolonged the life of the trees almost indefinitely. The oldest trees in a wood are likely to be the gnarled coppices and pollards rather than the stately standard trees. Some huge old coppice stools of hazel or ash may be over 500 years old. There are records of an ash stool in Suffolk that is 18 feet across. Its age is estimated at something over a 1,000 years, making it one of the oldest living things in Britain.

A use for every twig

For thousands of years trees and woodlands supplied men with the raw material for a vast number of tools and jobs. Houses and ships were built from the timber obtained from large trees, and smaller wood was used for fences, gates, in wattle and daub walls, in thatching, and of course for firewood. Clogs were made from alder wood, axe handles from ash, and in hard times the people might be reduced to eating the leaves of trees like elm. The undergrowth provided fodder for livestock in the form of leaves, small branches and fruit, like acorns, which were eagerly snuffled out by pigs in the winter months. Woods were a vital part of every country community and almost every leaf, fruit, twig and branch the wood produced was utilized in some way.

Many of the ancient woods, irregular in shape and rich in flora and fauna, did not change in shape or size for hundreds of years. Although their use may have changed, it was rare for woods to be grubbed out completely. It is only in the latter part of the 20th century that whole ancient woods have been destroyed on a large scale by physically grubbing out the root systems, and once the ancient and historic woods are lost they are lost for ever.

Roe deer
This is the British deer most associated with woodlands. It is a secretive animal, little more than two feet high at the shoulder, with a distinctive white rump patch that often gives away its position in woodland.

A roebuck

There are probably few woods in Scotland, the Lake District and southern England without a number of these enchanting creatures, but their shy habits are such that many people have never seen one. However, they are not wholly creatures of the woods, and can sometimes be seen feeding in open fields during the day.

Deer use paths that may have been used by their forebears for hundreds of years. These paths (called 'racks') can often be clearly seen leading across open country from one patch of woodland to another. Roe deer also give themselves away by their habit of stripping the bark off young trees to mark their territories. This often causes the tree to die or grow up deformed – one of the reasons why roe tend not to be popular with foresters. Other evidence of roe activity may be 'roe rings' made by the buck chasing the doe in circles during the courtship period, which lasts from mid-July to mid-August. The kids are born between April and June.

Below: a hazel coppice that is still cut on a regular basis. Hazel has a great number of uses, ranging from thatching spars to pea sticks. Left: a hazel stool with dog's mercury growing in the centre

Coniferous Woodlands

Winter sunlight casting long shadows in a Surrey pine wood

Red squirrel
Found in East Anglia, Wales, the Lake District and Scotland, the red squirrel is one of Britain's most enchanting native animals. It was once thought that the grey squirrel, which was introduced from America, would push the red from conifer woods as it had done from broad-leaved woodland, but the red squirrel is holding its own and may always have been better adapted to living in conifers.

Pine Marten
The pine marten is almost entirely confined to the forests of northern Scotland. It is a shy creature usually only active at night, but this is principally because of its fear of humans, and in quiet areas it can be seen hunting by day. It lives mainly on voles, mice, squirrels, rabbits and birds.

Since the formation of the Forestry Commission in 1919, hundreds of thousands of acres of mountain and moorland have been planted with various conifers. Planting entirely new woodlands was not an innovation – there are records of large-scale plantings from the 16th century – but the size of the undertaking (which still continues) has had far-reaching effects on the British countryside.

The conifer species most commonly grown are Norway spruce, sitka spruce, lodgepole pine, Douglas fir and various larches. Although the majority of the new woodlands have been created on treeless sites, many acres of broad-leaved woodland have also been replanted with quick-growing evergreens.

Few British animals are adapted to living with conifers, but in Scotland a number of mammals, notably deer, pine martens and wildcats have benefited from the protection afforded by the new forests. There are also indications that the polecat, once widespread but now largely confined to the uplands of Wales, has also increased in numbers because of the growth of conifer forests.

The new forests are supplying an increasing percentage of Britain's timber requirements, and many of them are also valuable recreational facilities in an overcrowded countryside; but they will never be as rich in wildlife as mixed broad-leaved woodland. Even so, forest rides, whether created as fire-breaks or as highways for forestry vehicles, can be valuable havens for wildlife, and in recent years efforts have been made to bring a greater diversity to one-species forests by the introduction of belts of deciduous trees and open areas. As the new forests reach maturity many of them will lose their dark and forbidding aspect as some areas are thinned and infilled with seedlings.

Native conifers

There are only three conifers native to Britain: Scots pine, yew and juniper. Juniper is more often thought of as a shrub, yet it can grow to a considerable height in favourable conditions. The berry-like fruits that it bears are in fact modified female cones – the male cones are like those on other conifers. Juniper can be found growing on chalk downland in parts of southern England and is fairly common in many forests in the Highlands of Scotland.

Yew is most often associated with churchyards, where some specimens attain very great age, but it can be found forming woods on chalk in the south, especially in Wiltshire, Hampshire and Sussex. Perhaps the most famous yew wood in Europe is at Kingley Vale in West Sussex; here gnarled old trees, perhaps 500 years old, cast such dense and impenetrable shade that nothing can grow beneath them.

Scots pine is common throughout Britain, but it can only be seen growing in something like its natural state in the Highlands of Scotland. Here the surviving remnants of huge forests that once covered most of Scotland have been carefully identified and conserved in recent years. These forest remnants are very different in appearance from modern conifer forests. The trees are generally widely spaced and are of many different shapes: some are thin and straight, some conical, and older specimens are often flat-topped.

In between the trees many different kinds of plants grow. Heathers are nearly always found, but bilberry, crowberry, bearberry and cowberry are often present. Common wild flowers are tormentil and heath bedstraw, while rarer beauties include lady's tresses orchid, twinflower, one-flowered wintergreen and chickweed wintergreen (which is actually a kind of primrose). Fungi are plentiful, and insects, though not as numerous as in broadleaved woods, are found in quite large numbers.

Scotland's two largest remaining Scots pine forests are the Black Wood of Rannoch and Rothiemurchus Forest, but smaller remnants can be found on Deeside, around Loch Maree, in Glen Affric and in the Glen More Forest Park.

Ancient yews marking a boundary of John O' Gaunts Deer Park at King's Somborne, Hampshire

Birds of conifer woods
Goldcrests, Britain's smallest birds, are found in nearly all coniferous woodland. Not so widespread are firecrests, distinguishable from goldcrests by their black eye-stripe, bold white stripe above that and brighter orange crown. Coal tits are the commonest tits in conifers; they can be distinguished from other black-capped tits by the white patch that runs from the back of their heads down to the nape of the neck. One of the most distinctive finches in conifers is the siskin. This little green bird prefers well-grown woodland.

A female goldcrest

Three birds are confined to the pine forests of Scotland. The most charming of these is the crested tit, a rare bird that is entirely confined to ancient pine woods. Before the forests were destroyed it may have been quite common, but it declined as its habitat disappeared, and it seems incapable of colonizing new areas. The crossbill has specially adapted mandibles which enable it to extract the seeds from pine cones. The Scottish crossbill is a distinct sub-species from the common crossbill that is often seen in East Anglia and southern England. Capercaillies cannot be mistaken for any other bird. Approaching turkeys in size, male capercaillies have dark plumage, fan tails, and a call which sounds very much like a cork being drawn from a bottle. They can be belligerent, and have been known to launch themselves at people.

The Countryside at Night

Right: the main picture is of a pipistrelle, the most common British bat. Inset are barn owls at a nest (left), a nightingale (top right) and a badger (bottom right)

The nightingale

Perhaps the most celebrated of British songsters, nightingales arrive in this country (where they are confined to England south and east of a line between the Severn and the Humber) in the spring and set up their territories in woods and hedges with dense undergrowth. Contrary to popular misconception, nightingales sing at any time of day or night, but their extraordinary repertoire of beautiful, rising song interspersed with a bizarre mixture of whistles, churrs and croaks, is best appreciated on quiet evenings. Shy birds, nightingales are seldom seen, preferring to sing from deep in the foliage. The nest of dead leaves, lined with grass and hair, is built on or near the ground and may contain six eggs. The singing ceases when the young are born in June.

Earthworms

Earthworms, of which there are very many different sorts, form a large part of the diet of many of the animals that are active at night.

Several kinds of earthworm, notably *Lumbricus terrestris*, emerge from their burrows on warm, damp summer evenings to feed and to mate. These worms stretch most of their length over the grass near their burrows, but keep their tail ends very firmly anchored in the burrow so that they can draw back in quickly if danger threatens. Active worms can react astonishingly quickly both to vibrations and to light.

The most commonly seen worm-hunters are hedgehogs. If approached quietly with a torch they will continue about their business seemingly undisturbed by the light. Hedgehogs are as likely to be heard as seen – their scuffling through the undergrowth is often accompanied by pig-like squeals – an explanation for their name.

Foxes and badgers also take large numbers of worms; indeed some studies have shown that the diet of foxes consists largely of these and other small invertebrates.

As TWILIGHT falls over the countryside a large number of creatures rarely seen during the day become active. With care and patience many of these can be watched with comparative ease; the most important rules for watching the larger animals are always to be quiet and always to be downwind of them. Nearly all animals rely on hearing and smell far more than humans do; but as the light decreases their sight becomes more acute than ours.

Foxes

Present in large numbers throughout Britain, foxes are most often seen as shadows in the light of a car headlamp, or as distant shapes seen flitting across a field.

Foxes are most active at night, and frequently cover large distances under cover of darkness. The best place to watch fox activity is at an earth (the name given to a foxes' home) during the evening or early morning when cubs are present. Cubs are usually born at the end of March, and for several weeks they are confined to the earth by their mother. But after about a month they begin to spend time at the entrance to the earth, and by early summer they will make quite long expeditions from the earth. Cubs are far less wary than their parents, and it is often possible to watch them for long periods without causing them alarm. However, if the vixen becomes nervous she will move the cubs to another earth.

One of the most spine-chilling of all night-time sounds is that of courting foxes in December and January. Foxes have a variety of calls, but the blood-curdling screech of the vixen is by far the most dramatic. It is believed this call may be made by the vixen to attract dog foxes when she is on heat, although many naturalists now think that the scream is also uttered by dog foxes. Vixens also utter the screaming note in early summer to communicate with cubs. Fox activity can be traced during the day by following footprints in snow or mud. These trails will often reveal well-used paths and distinct territories. Droppings and urine are used to mark territorial boundaries. The strong acrid smell often encountered on a country walk can sometimes be traced to a fox's territory marker.

Badgers

Even less commonly seen than foxes, Badgers are in fact widely distributed throughout Britain. Their tunnel systems, or setts, are usually found in woods, copses and thick hedges. Badgers are creatures of habit, and may have used the same setts and pathways for hundreds, or even thousands, of years. Such well-established setts may cover considerable areas. Some setts, however, are only occupied intermittently.

Badgers emerge from the sett in the late evening, and one of their first actions is to visit the latrines which they excavate near to the tunnel entrance. They also like a drink, and paths may lead to a stream or pool. Badgers are extremely clean animals, and a sure sign that a sett is inhabited will be piles of discarded bedding just outside the tunnel entrance. Badgers are born between mid-January and mid-March, but their eyes are closed for the first five weeks of life, and they do not venture out of the sett for several weeks after they can see. They begin to emerge in April and May, when they are weaned, and this is the best time to go badger-watching.

Bats

True creatures of the night, bats emerge from their daytime resting places at twilight to hunt for moths and other night-flying insects. Bats are rarely seen close enough to distinguish different species, but the one most commonly seen in Britain is the pipistrelle. Over 15 different species have been recorded in Britain; most of these are rare and all seem to be decreasing in numbers. Viewed with suspicion and fear by many, they are harmless creatures that are beneficial to man because of the large numbers of insect pests that they eat. They are especially useful in destroying death watch beetles and woodworm beetles in old buildings.

Glow-worms

The pale green light shed by glow-worms is one of the most charming night-time sights. Both sexes emit the light, but that from the adult female is stronger. She is a flightless creature looking not unlike a woodlouse, but the male has wings and wing cases like any other beetle. Glow-worms feed on snails, which they eat by injecting fluids which dissolve them; they then suck the juices. Grassy banks on chalk and limestone are the best places to look for glow-worms, but they are not widespread.

Owls

Of the 11 species of owl that have been recorded in Britain, the two most commonly seen and heard night-flyers are the tawny owl and the barn owl.

Tawny owls are only active at night, when their hunting *kee-vit* calls can be heard throughout much of Britain. The famous *tu-whit-tu-whoo* is in fact made by two birds; the male calls *tu-whoo*, and the female may reply with the call note (*kerwick* or *ky-whit*), mainly in spring. Often seen floating by on silent white wings, the barn owl hunts by day as well as by night. Resident throughout Britain, barn owls often call in a piercing scream when on the wing.

Barn owls are far less common than they were, largely because many die after eating rats and mice contaminated by poisons. Generally speaking, barn owls are birds of relatively open farmland, while tawny owls are largely found in woodland.

The Mountains

Mountain landscapes

TOWERING mountain peaks provide the wildest scenery in Britain. The most spectacular mountains are found in north Wales, the Lake District and the Highlands and Islands of Scotland. In these areas rain, snow, frost and wind are the dominant forces.

All of our mountain ranges have been subject to periods of glaciation that lasted for millions of years. The great corries and U-shaped valleys of north Wales, for instance, were formed by the gouging action of glaciers rolling down from the vast ice sheets then covering Snowdonia's central massif. The history of the Lake District is similar; here Helvellyn is at the centre of an enormous dome from which radiate lake-filled valleys scraped out by the ice as it ground its inexorable way down the slopes. The action of the weather over millions of years has worn down the summits of Britain's mountains; none are now high enough to be snow-covered all the year, though snow does lie in sheltered places well into the year on the highest ranges.

Many of the highest peaks are rugged and broken, partly as a result of the ice-sheets plucking massive chunks from them, and partly through the action of severe frosts, which gradually broke and crumbled the rock, often resulting in scree slopes of broken material. Rain has played its part, and continues to do so; the mountains are still being slowly washed into the sea.

Mountain plants

The peaks of the highest mountains may at first sight appear devoid of all life, but even in these inhospitable conditions lichens and mosses can be found. The lichens play an important role in barren places, for as they spread across the rocks the surface gradually powders away, eventually creating tiny pockets of loose material in which other plants can grow.

Alpine flowers grow in some localities, and one sort at least, starry saxifrage, occurs on the summit of Ben Nevis, Britain's highest mountain. Such flowers are specially adapted for living in harsh conditions. Many have a spreading habit, so that the wind is less likely to dislodge them or dry them out; some are cushion-shaped in order to conserve both warmth and moisture; and others are succulents with fleshy leaves and stems that can conserve moisture in the drying winds that sweep continually across the rocks.

Various grasses are the dominant plants on many lower slopes and mountains. The most common are the *Nardus* grasses like mat grass. Others include sheep's fescue and purple moor grass. Moorland plants of various kinds form the most widespread plant communities in nearly all upland regions (see pages 32–33 for moorland).

Once hunted almost to extinction, wildcats control the numbers of small mammals that would otherwise damage young trees and are now welcomed in some areas

Wildcat

Although similar in appearance to a large tabby, the wildcat is not related to domestic cats but belongs to an entirely different species. Wildcats now live only in the Highlands of Scotland (though they are thought to be spreading southwards), but were once common throughout Britain. They spend most of the day resting and are most active at dawn and dusk. Their prey consists largely of rabbits, hares and mice, but they will take a great variety of other creatures if the opportunity arises. Wildcats are ferocious if cornered, but are frightened of men and dogs and will always try to avoid a confrontation.

Wild goats

Wild goats are descended either from domestic goats that escaped captivity, or from small numbers deliberately released. Some of the herds may have been roaming free for hundreds of years. The goats are usually seen on steep crags and display an astonishing agility in these hazardous terrains. This is partly explained by their hooves, which act like suction pads when they come into contact with rock, attaching the goat firmly to its foothold. Wild goats can be seen in parts of Snowdonia, and there are scattered herds throughout Scotland.

Mountain Wildlife

NE of the most rewarding ways to see upland wildlife is to walk up the banks of a mountain stream. A great variety of mosses, ferns and grasses thrive in the wet conditions, and trees such as rowan and birch grow on steep slopes that are inaccessible to sheep. Wildflowers like primroses, usually associated with woodlands, can often be found in these sheltered conditions.

Heathers are often dominant on lower upland slopes, but grasses cover huge areas of many regions. In boggy places sphagnum and other mosses make up the major plant communities, perhaps with coarse grasses and sedges. Alpine flowers and plants can be found in some mountainous areas.

Upland birds

Apart from sheep, birds are the creatures most likely to be seen in Britain's uplands.

Buzzards are fairly common in all upland areas. Their plaintive mewing call often gives their position away as they soar high in the sky taking advantage of every current of air. Buzzards also spend a good deal of time perched on trees, posts and telegraph poles, and at such times people in cars may obtain excellent views of them, for they do not associate cars with humans and will remain on their perches for quite long periods with the car very close.

Dippers are enchanting birds to watch. They are always found on or near fast-flowing upland streams, and the presence of a dipper on a stretch of water can often be detected from white droppings on exposed rocks in water. If disturbed, dippers will fly away very fast, always close to the surface of the water. However, they have relatively small territories, so they do not fly far, and soon return if all seems quiet. They are unique among perching birds in that they wade along the bed of streams and can feed under water. Dippers often nest on ledges under the protective canopy of a waterfall.

Ravens are usually found where there are steep crags and precipitous cliffs. It is in such places, or in tall trees, that they build their nests. These huge birds, which look so ungainly on the ground, are masters of the air and perform dazzling aerobatic feats, including flying upside down for quite considerable periods.

Often seen on Scotland's wild and treeless

mountain slopes, the ptarmigan is a member of the grouse family. It can be distinguished from the red grouse by its white wings and underparts. Ptarmigans moult three times in the year; in spring and summer they are light brown with grey underparts; for a brief period in autumn they become very much greyer all over; and in winter they become completely white. These changes of colour coincide almost exactly with changes in the terrain in which they live, so ptarmigans are well disguised all the year round.

Golden plovers breed on upland moors from Devon to the Scottish Islands, but are much more widespread in winter, when they can be found in many lowland localities. Their nests are difficult to find because the eggs are camouflaged, and because a bird leaving the nest will run long distances before taking flight. If a nest is approached both male and female plover fly round the intruder making distressed calls, and long after the danger has passed the birds will stand on the ground uttering a single mournful note that seems at times to contain the very essence of all wild and desolate places.

Key

1 Ptarmigan
2 Woolly hair moss
3 Mountain fern
4 Moss campion (*July–August*)
5 Crowberry (*April–June*)
6 Bilberry (*April–June*)
7 Mountain ash (*also known as rowan*)
8 Buzzard
9 Heather (*July–September*)
10 Starry saxifrage (*June–August*)
11 Dipper
12 Wheatear (*Summer visitor*)
13 Cotton grass
14 Heather
15 Sphagnum moss
16 Golden plover
17 Black-faced sheep
18 Raven
19 Meadow pipit
20 Purple moor grass
21 Wavy hair grass
22 Sheep's fescue

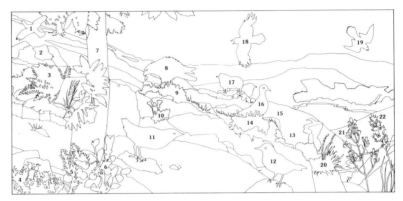

The plants and animals are not drawn to scale. Plants are in flower during the months shown in brackets

Lakes and Reservoirs

Right: glacial Wastwater, set in the heart of the Lake District, is the deepest natural lake in England. The screes support little vegetation; even parsley fern and bilberry, plants adapted to colonizing bare scree, have made little progress on these steep rocky slopes, where often only lichens and mosses can grow

Below: Craig Goch is one of the Elan Valley complex of reservoirs

Man-made lakes
From Victorian times onward, reservoirs have been created to supply the ever-increasing demands of domestic and industrial water-users. Some of the most famous are those that form the Elan Valley complex west of Rhayader in mid Wales. These huge undertakings, which supply Birmingham with water, drowned some of the wildest and most remote scenery in western Britain. Although a mixed blessing from a naturalist's point of view, they are popular tourist attractions and undoubtedly give pleasure to many.

As with natural lakes, it is the shallow reservoirs in fertile areas that are the richest in wildlife. The banks of these waters are often carpeted with wild plants like purple loosestrife, flags, flowering rush, and willowherbs. Beautiful lakes in exquisite settings can be found in the grounds of stately homes created by such landscape artists as Capability Brown in the 18th and 19th centuries.

Some of the most recent lakes, often created inadvertently, are the drowned excavations of gravel and clay pits. Many of these are now public areas, and where leisure activities are controlled these can become valuable refuges for water-loving birds of many kinds and also for thousands of insects and a variety of mammals.

Lakes and reservoirs

NATURAL lakes contribute immensely to the beauty of Britain. The deep, cold lakes of the upland regions are often inhospitable to wildlife, but shallow waters and lowland lakes form some of the country's richest habitats. The creation of hundreds of reservoirs since Victorian times has added new water habitats, while water-filled gravel pits and other flooded excavations have to some extent compensated for the natural wetland and water sites lost through drainage and agricultural improvement – sites which are among the most threatened habitats in Britain.

The Highlands of Scotland, the Lake District and north Wales contain most of Britain's largest and deepest lakes. Nearly all of these were formed in the huge valleys scraped out of the rock by glaciers during the ice ages. Such lakes are often too deep and too cold to support many kinds of life. They also frequently occur on hard, acidic rocks that release few of the nutrients essential for plant life to survive. Even the shores of these upland lakes may support little life, since winds cause waves which repeatedly wash up and down, constantly moving the silt deposited on the shoreline and creating an unstable environment in which plant life has little chance of setting seed, taking root and establishing itself.

When such lakes were first formed they were rich in nutrients and silts left in the lake bottoms by the melting ice and washed off the surrounding land by rain. But as time passed, the remaining nutrients in the land were washed out, and the nutrients in the water were used up by plants and animals, eventually starving the lakes and leaving them devoid of life. In the last 200 years, man has affected some of these lakes. Agricultural activity has increased in some areas,

Great crested grebe
During the breeding season, which begins in February, great crested grebes have some of the most spectacular plumage of all water birds. At this time both sexes have crests and neck ruffs. These are fluffed out during the courtship displays, which consist of much head-shaking and diving. The most extraordinary part of the display occurs when the pair approach each other breast to breast, with most of their bodies raised clear of the water, and present each other with offerings of vegetation.

Great crested grebes prefer to live and breed in large expanses of water with thick vegetation in which to make their nests, but they can also be seen on relatively bare reservoirs. Their numbers have greatly increased in recent years through the appearance of large numbers of water-filled gravel pits.

Ducks
Ducks can be seen in thousands on some lakes, especially in the winter months. Among the best places for wildfowl are reservoirs like Grafham Water near Huntingdon, Rutland Water near Oakham and those near Heathrow Airport in London.

Dabbling ducks, like mallard and teal, are restricted by their feeding habits to shallow waters, but the diving ducks, of which pochard and tufted ducks are by far the most common, can be seen in lakes and reservoirs with quite deep water.

The pochard is about 18 inches long, and the drake is easily distinguished from other ducks by his plumage of grey body, black breast and dark red head.

Tufted ducks are about the same size as pochards, but their outline and plumage is quite different. The drakes have dark purple plumage with a white flash along the flanks and bright yellow eyes. Both drake and duck have the tufts on their heads which give them their name. Both species of duck breed in eastern Europe in large numbers, and many of these spend the winter in Britain.

providing nutrients, and sewage has tended to enter the water, also bringing nutrients. In more recent times inorganic fertilizers have been washed off the land into the water, adding chemicals such as nitrogen and phosphates. Examples of both types of lakes can be seen in the Lake District. Buttermere is in a thinly populated area with poor soils, and has little life, whereas Esthwaite Water receives water drained off agricultural soils and supports a variety of plants and animals.

Retreating glaciers created other types of lakes that are naturally rich in life. Examples of these can be found in Shropshire, where hundreds of small lakes were created when slow-melting ice was surrounded by gravel, sand and clay deposited by ice that melted more quickly. The resulting hollows, or kettle holes, became shallow lakes. Some of these meres – as they are known – are now covered by vegetation.

Shallow lakes with gently sloping sides surrounded by fertile land are the richest in life. These occur mainly in lowland Britain. Such lakes can sometimes be threatened by too many nutrients entering them. The nutrients encourage algae, which although they give off oxygen during the day consume it at night, and large concentrations of algal growth, called blooms, can be so all-consuming that they destroy all life in the water.

Rivers and Streams

Upland streams

MOUNTAIN streams are usually fast-flowing and cold. Very few creatures are able to survive in such streams because they would be quickly dislodged by the current. Plants are also excluded by the current, and by the stony beds of upland streams, which offer them no foothold. However, where these streams form quiet pools and shallows some invertebrates are able to find food and make their homes.

Streams at lower levels do not flow so fast, and are joined by tributaries that bring in nutrients and silts. The flow may still be too fast for many plants, but the silts and debris that have fallen to the river bed and accumulated in slack shallows at the streamside provide shelter for numbers of invertebrates. Such places are favourite hunting grounds for the common sandpiper, a small summer-visiting wader with white underparts and a brown back. Trout live in waters that would be too fast for other fish; they can swim against the current and prefer highly oxygenated water.

Chalk streams

Streams flowing from chalk are greatly affected by the dissolved calcium that they carry. In such streams water snails, which require calcium to build their shells, are often abundant. Leeches may also be present in these waters. Many slow chalk streams in southern England have been widened and ducted to form watercress beds. These beds can be superb places to watch wagtails, ducks, snipe, redshanks and other waders. Large rivers like the Itchen and the Test in Hampshire have their sources in chalk, and their lower reaches are regarded as the finest trout-fishing waters in Britain.

Lowland rivers

Rivers flowing through flat countryside are usually slow, and this enables many plants to take root in the silts and debris that are constantly being brought down from the upper reaches. The large number of plants attract insects, and these provide food for other insects, fishes and animals. The water at the banks of slow rivers may be almost still, and here rushes, reeds and other water-loving plants grow, creating more habitats and causing further silting of the river. Rivers always take the easiest route to the sea, not the quickest, so rivers in flat country may take tortuous, meandering courses, often ending up in a series of great loops. Sometimes the loops join up, and ox-bow lakes are formed. Especially slow rivers with a high silt content may be so dark and poor in oxygen that only a few determined bottom-feeding fish, like bream, can survive in the murky conditions.

Crayfishing

On the Continent, crayfish are regarded as a delicacy, but in Britain few people eat them despite the fact that they are as tasty as lobsters. Crayfish are found in fairly shallow streams and rivers where the water is clean and there is not too much vegetation. They like to make their homes in soft banks, but will also live beneath tree roots or under stones. Crayfish look like small lobsters, and like lobsters they change colour when cooked.

The traditional time to catch crayfish is at night in autumn when they are most active. Rotten fish is tied to the centre of a circular drop-net which is carefully lowered into the stream with the aid of a long pole. After about ten minutes the net is raised, and with any luck crayfish will have been attracted onto the net by the bait. A less dignified way of catching crayfish is simply to scoop them out of their hiding places under the bank with bare hands.

The waters of the River Wharfe in North Yorkshire are aptly described by the name of the gorge through which it flows – Strid Gorge. Strid is the Old English word for turmoil

Wagtails

Three species of wagtail are common in Britain, and all are typical birds of rivers and water. Of these the pied wagtail is the most numerous and is found in a great variety of habitats. It has black and white plumage that becomes shot with grey in winter. Grey and yellow wagtails are often confused, but the grey is blue-grey above, pale yellow beneath and has a yellow-green rump, while the yellow has a bright yellow face, neck and underparts and is greenish-brown above. All the wagtails live on insects, but there are slight variations in their feeding habits. The yellow, for instance, often searches for insects disturbed by cattle, but the grey is much more dependent on creatures found in or near water. The pied is very catholic in its tastes, and will come to bird tables in severe winters. Pied wagtails are found all over Britain, as is the grey, but the yellow, which is a summer visitor, is not often seen in Scotland. Yellow wagtails arrive in this country in April and leave for southern Africa, where they spend the winter, in October.

55

A Lowland River

HE illustration shows a cross-section through a slow-flowing lowland river. Silts and decaying vegetable matter have built up alongside the banks, enabling a rich flora to develop. Water beetles and bugs like the whirligig and the water boatman are found in still water where the current cannot carry them away. Both live on other insects and water creatures – the water boatman being a ferocious hunter quite capable of delivering a bite to humans. Moorhens and coots are common throughout Britain and are easy to watch, but the dabchick (or little grebe) is much more elusive since it dives whenever alarmed. However, it surfaces nearby not long afterwards, sometimes in the middle of a patch of weeds.

The plants and animals are not drawn to scale. Plants are in flower during the months shown in brackets

Estuaries and Salt Marshes

BRITAIN is particularly rich in estuarine environments. They can be found all round the coast from the north of Scotland to the Cornish peninsula. Perhaps the most rewarding times to visit estuaries are autumn and winter, when they become temporary homes for thousands of wildfowl, waders and seabirds.

Nearly all estuaries have been created by slowly rising sea levels drowning the lowest reaches of river valleys. Most of the plants and animals found in estuarine habitats are specially adapted to life in very saline conditions. They also need to be able to adapt rapidly from relatively fresh water at low tide to high concentrations of salt at high tide. This applies especially to bottom-living fish like dabs and flounders, since salt water is heavier than fresh and the saltiest water is nearest the estuary floor. The mudflats in estuaries may look uninviting and sterile, but in fact they are teeming with invertebrate life and it is this which attracts the birds during the winter months.

It was long ago realized that the silts of estuaries and mudflats were particularly rich in nutrients, and as early as Roman times walls were built to keep the waters out. Most of this reclaimed land was used as pasture, and when pasture like this has not been treated with selective weedkillers and fertilizers it can be rich in grasses and certain flowers. Grazing by cattle controlled the growth of scrub, and thus preserved the open aspect. Coincidentally these pastures provide superb feeding grounds for ducks and geese. As pressure from seaside development increases, and ploughing becomes more and more widespread, these ancient pastures, which may still have clearly visible dry gullies where the estuarine waters once flowed, are increasingly threatened.

Salt marshes

These usually develop along the lowest levels of rivers or where areas of flat land are sheltered from moving water – behind either a natural barrier or a man-made sea wall. The first colonizers of such places are usually green seaweeds, eel grass, or cord grass – a plant which originated in Southampton Water in the 19th century when two grasses, one from America, hybridized. Since that time cord grass has spread all round the coast. The next colonizer may be glasswort, a fleshy plant which bears tiny yellow flowers.

These plants encourage further growth of the mudbanks, in between which deep channels develop. Along these sea-purslane may grow. This plant, which has tufts of yellow flowers, is protected from the drying effects of sea-water and wind by scales that cover its leaves. These retain a layer of moist air against the leaf surface, and reflect the sun's rays. As further consolidation of the silts and muds takes place, sea-lavender, sea-aster and thrift often become abundant in areas washed only by high tides. Sea-rushes and reeds grow in areas only reached by the highest tides.

Key

1 Greater black-backed gull
2 Sea purslane
  (*July–September*)
3 Heron
4 Sea lavender
  (*July–September*)
5 Shelduck
6 Glasswort (*also known as marsh samphire; August–September*)
7 Oystercatcher
8 Black-headed gull
9 Sanderling
10 Redshank
11 Little stint
12 Knot
13 Curlew
14 Knot
15 Dunlin

The plants and birds are not drawn to scale. Plants are in flower during the months shown in brackets. All the birds are shown in their summer plumage

The Seashore

Sandwood Bay, on the north-west coast of Scotland, combines many seashore habitats – rocks, rock pools, beaches and dunes – with the influence of a small tidal river

Seals

Two species of seal, the Atlantic and the grey, live and breed in British coastal waters. Both are usually seen only as they float, heads out of the water, a little way offshore. Closer views, often of seals basking, can be obtained from boats that visit their breeding grounds. The two species can sometimes be distinguished by the shape of their heads, as grey seals have longer, more pointed noses. Grey seals breed mainly on the Farne Islands, the Outer Hebrides and the Orkneys. There are also small colonies off the coast of Pembrokeshire. Grey seal pups are born in autumn and winter. The largest concentration of Atlantic seals is found in the Wash, and they also breed in the Hebrides, Orkneys and Shetlands. Atlantic seal pups are born in June and July. Outside the breeding season seals can be seen around many parts of the coast; they have even occasionally been seen in the Thames at London!

EXPLORING Britain's varied coastline by walking the magnificent coastal paths established in recent years, or simply lying on beaches soaking up the sun, are two ways in which the seaside may be enjoyed. Although the active walker may see a greater variety of wildlife, the passive sunbather may discover quite large numbers of creatures living under the sand all around him.

Sandy and muddy shores

At low tide the animals that live permanently in sand or mud either hide under stones or bury themselves, often deeply. As the tide returns and covers the beach, small sea creatures and plant materials are washed in, and fish and crustaceans move in to take advantage of the food supplies.

Lugworms are some of the commonest creatures living in muddy foreshores. A lugworm's position can be easily detected by casts of undigested material that has passed through the animal's gut and is expelled onto the surface. Nearby will be a slight depression which marks the place where the lugworm, which lives in a U-shaped burrow, sucks in food material. Fan worms live in tubes which they construct with sand particles. When the tide comes in the worms extend delicate, wavy tentacles into the water. These collect food and more sand for tube building. Empty tubes can often be found in shallow pools on sandy shores. Great numbers of bivalve molluscs like cockles live in the sand and soft mud. They feed by means of tubes called siphons which they extend up through the sand or mud to the water, where one siphon sucks in clear water and food, while the other expels used water and detritus. Razor shells live in clean sand. Sometimes they can be seen protruding

In sands such as these at Birling Gap on the south coast, although often crowded with holidaymakers in summer, can be found the flora and fauna common to most of the British coastline

Sand dunes
These occur when wind-blown dry sand is driven inshore until it reaches an obstruction; small mounds of sand build up and these may be colonized first by sea couch grass and then by marram grass. Marram grass has the ability to survive being completely covered by sand, so it goes on growing up through newly blown sand, and the dunes gradually increase in size. As the marram grass, and other early colonizers like sea bindweed, become established, they in turn supply suitable conditions for other plants.

The plant life that eventually develops is dependent on the composition of the sand; if it has lots of lime-rich shell fragments in it a community of lime-loving plants will develop; if the sand is composed entirely of quartz particles it will be acidic, and plants typical of heathland will grow up.

It is possible in some large dunelands to see a complete succession from bare sand, to marram-covered dunes, to a thick ground flora, and, well away from the open sea, scrub thickets and even trees, most often birch, pine, or willow.

The sandhopper, a night feeder, spends the day under the sand, but is easily disturbed by passers-by

above the surface, but they can detect slight vibrations and can quickly withdraw into the sand by means of muscular action.

Sand-eels lie just under the surface at low tide, as do masked crabs, which take in oxygenated water by means of antennae that protrude above the sand. The burrowing starfish sinks into the sand in search of its prey of worms and molluscs.

Shingle banks and beaches
Shingle accumulates at the top of beaches, and there is often sand at a lower level. This is because waves have tremendous driving energy as they surge inshore, but their power is greatly decreased as they reach the top of the beach so pebbles and shingle are left behind, while smaller particles are carried back by the outgoing waves.

Many shingle beaches are unstable and in constant motion, so that plants cannot become established, but in places away from the direct action of the sea plants like sea beet, orache, shrubby sea blite and sea campion grow. Such plants are adapted for salty environments, and have deep roots that can probe the shingle for fresh water. Wading birds often come to feed on the water margins of stable shingle beaches when their muddy feeding grounds are covered by the tide.

When shingle drifts across the mouth of a river, huge bars like the one at Spurn Head in Humberside are often created. Although such bars often look stable and have a covering of vegetation, they are always shifting and Spurn Head is constantly changing in shape and size. Shingle banks sometimes build up offshore parallel with the mainland, and these may eventually join the mainland at each end, creating lagoons like the one behind Chesil Beach in Dorset.

The tideline
Huge quantities of material are cast on to beaches at each high tide. Much of this is seaweed and other vegetable matter carried from the sea bed, but there may also be shore crabs, fishes caught unawares by the tide, and many shells. The edible material is very soon devoured by seabirds, and by huge numbers of tiny invertebrates. These include sandhoppers, bristle-tails, springtails and various kinds of fly. Man-made flotsam and jetsam of every description is always present, sometimes including items of value, which only dedicated beach-combers prepared to set out at dawn are likely to find.

Cliffs and Rock Pools

HATTERED and sculpted by constant wave action, cliffs occur round the coast of much of Britain. They are mostly composed of sedimentary rocks like shales, clays, limestones and sandstones, but there are rugged cliffs of granite at Land's End, while some of the magnificent cliffs in the Highlands and Islands of Scotland are of rocks laid down in very early geological periods.

The wildlife communities of cliffs are determined by the rocks of which they are composed, and by the climate and prevailing weather conditions. Plants growing on cliff sites are constantly exposed to high concentrations of salt and strong winds. Many of these plants have become specially adapted to survive in such conditions. Thrift, for example, has very deep roots and grows in dense, spongy cushions that hug the ground, enabling it to conserve moisture in the drying winds. Thrift also has narrow leaves that help it to reduce water loss. Other plants conserve moisture by having waxy leaves – sea campion is one example – or by having succulent leaves like the English stonecrop.

Plants like thrift and sea campion are often found growing in short turf on cliff-tops. Another cliff-top plant, found on northern and western shores, is vernal squill, which has a group of delicate blue flowers. Bluebells may be found on more sheltered cliff-tops, perhaps growing in amongst rocky outcrops.

Further down the cliff face, where the concentrations of salt spray are much higher, fewer plants are found. Two of these are rock samphire, an edible plant once widely used in pickles and salads, and wild cabbage, an ancestor of many cultivated cabbages. Lower still may be found sea beet, the wild ancestor of beetroot and other vegetables. In places constantly splashed by the sea only specially adapted lichens may grow.

Birds can contribute to the diversity of plants on cliffs. Their droppings supply valuable nutrients, but large concentrations will kill even the most resilient plants. Birds inhabit specific zones on cliffs, so that, for example, puffins make their nests in burrows on cliff tops, while kittiwakes build their nests on ledges on the cliff face. Shags and cormorants spend much of their time on rocks near the water's edge, but tend to build their nests on ledges higher up. The eggs of many seabirds are long with pointed ends; this shape greatly decreases the likelihood of the eggs rolling off cliffs.

Rock pools

There are a great many different kinds of rock pools, and the diversity of animal and plant life that they contain varies considerably. Pools well away from the sea may be filled with sea-water only occasionally, and are often very saline. At other times they fill with rain water and the salt is diluted. They are also subject to considerable temperature changes. For these reasons they are usually poor in life. Shallow pools nearer the sea tend to dry out quickly, and any animals washed into them by the tide are usually snapped up by seabirds. The richest pools are usually those found in sheltered rocky gullies, and deep pools very close to the water's edge which are constantly replenished by fresh sea-water.

Key
1 Herring gull
2 Cormorant
3 Turnstone
4 Mermaid's purse (*egg-case of dogfish*)
5 Mussels
6 Limpets
7 Winkles
8 Shanny
9 Common shore crab
10 Bladderwrack
11 Common star fish
12 Common prawn
13 Hermit crab
14 *Corallina officinalis*
15 Sea lettuce
16 Sea anemone
17 Shag
18 Cormorant
19 Sea campion (*June–September*)
20 Kittiwake
21 Thrift (*March–October*)

The plants and animals are not drawn to scale. Plants are in flower during the months shown in brackets

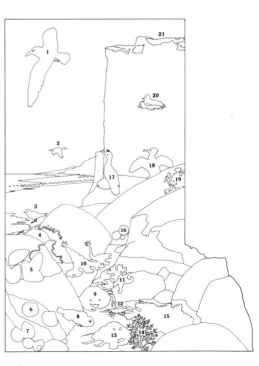

Lanes and Paths

EXPLORING quiet lanes is a delightful experience that may reveal a wealth of wildlife as well as glimpses of lovely scenery through gateways and over hedgerows. Footpaths are in more direct and intimate contact with the countryside. They may wander across fields, meadows, moorlands or heaths for mile upon mile, perhaps never passing near a village or house. Footpaths came into being for specific purposes, and although some may appear to have no discernible goal today, study of a large-scale map will often reveal their original destination.

The Ridgeway, a prehistoric trackway which is now one of the finest long-distance footpaths in the country, at Barbury Castle, a hill-fort near Wroughton in Wiltshire

Verges
Many roadside verges, once ignored or sprayed with herbicides by county councils who thought they looked tidier without foaming cow parsley in spring or poppies in summer, are now recognized as valuable wildlife habitats. It really does pay to stop the car and take a stroll along any country road, just to look at a stretch of what seems to be ordinary grass verge. Even if you are speeding along a motorway, you will surprised by the rich delights now apparent on many motorway embankments. Small mammals quickly get used to traffic, undisturbed by any other human movement, and wild plants—sometimes with help from county councils or local people—swiftly colonize the once bulldozed earth. The small animals, principally voles, attract kestrels; and invertebrates, including worms coaxed out of the earth by traffic vibration, tempt magpies and other members of the crow family to explore verges and hard shoulders.

Ancient trackways
The first trackways were formed across the ridges of the southern downlands of England some 4,000 years ago, during the Neolithic period. They were the first true highways. The sea and rivers were important routes, but their estuaries and valleys were often densely wooded and marshy. The best alternatives for driving cattle and sheep, for carrying the produce of cornfield or flintmine, even for bearing the dead to such great tombs as Hetty Pegler's Tump in the Cotswolds, were the thinly-wooded uplands.

Many old trackways became well established, like the Icknield Way from Norfolk to the south coast, or the Berkshire Ridgeway which passes the ancient Uffington White Horse carved in the chalk below. Some were later used as part of the system of drove roads along which cattle and sheep were driven out of Wales and Scotland and from all parts of England to the great medieval markets. Such drove roads, or 'drifts', are often marked by pub signs like The Drover's Arms. Sometimes animals were driven to summer grazing along local drove roads, resulting in village names like Drove End. Mostly abandoned with the coming of the railways in the 19th century, some became green lanes, like many ancient tracks or medieval boundaries: wide, hedgy paths that often seem to go nowhere, or downland ways ringing with the song of skylarks, rippled with corn or bright with wild thyme, vetches and orchids.

Whenever a lane is flanked by walls or hedges at some distance from the edge of the road, it is a sign that the drovers used to pass that way. The wide verges may have been for wayside grazing, which was sometimes permitted.

The Harroway was one of the great prehistoric trackways, and parts of it, like this stretch near Andover in Hampshire, are included in the modern road system

Roman roads and medieval routes

Because they tend not to pass through or near present-day towns and villages, fewer of the ancient trackways have been incorporated into modern roads than the arrow-straight Roman roads. Skilled surveyors and engineers built this great network, linking such Roman centres as Lincoln, York and Winchester. They were metalled, drained and cambered. Many of our roads today have a Roman foundation, like the Fosse Way or Watling Street, which bear their original local names. Names are often evocative. The many Salt Ways and Saltfords are reminders of the old packhorse routes from seaside salt pans or the boiling brine pits at such places as Droitwich in Worcestershire, famous for its salt for some 2,000 years. Medieval pilgrims trod the Pilgrims' Ways like the one south of Guildford, between Winchester and Canterbury.

Country roads

The dense web of country roads which form a complex pattern within these main routes came into being through a long and seemingly haphazard process. When the Roman legions left Britain in the 5th century to defend what was left of the Empire, some sections were still used and the salt ways and drove roads remained important, but most people retreated to small rural communities which were largely self-sufficient, and required only local trackways. To go to market, to church or to pasture his cow the countryman might go by way of a ford, round a patch of forest, avoiding a steep hill and the cultivated strips of his neighbours.

Each parish was responsible for repairing the roads within its own boundary, but few did so. Not until the Turnpike Trusts were set up from the end of the 17th century was anything done about the state of the roads. Each trust was established by Act of Parliament and raised money for repairing and even building highways through tolls taken at turnpikes. Many of the tollhouses can be seen along the roads today, often in neo-Gothic or early Victorian picturesque styles, reflecting the taste of the local gentry who made up the boards of trustees. Altogether the Turnpike Trusts built or repaired about 22,000 miles of road, although they remained potholed and rutted until the early 19th century, when Scottish engineers Thomas Telford and John Macadam used graded broken stones to form a compacted surface. A few years later tar was mixed with the stones to create Tarmacadam.

Today there are over 210,000 miles of public highway in Great Britain, of which some 1,600 are motorways built within the last 25 years. One of their great benefits has been to free the minor roads of heavy traffic, so that it is still possible to turn down a quiet country lane and find rich rewards.

Footpaths

The word 'path' comes from an Old English word meaning to pad, or tread. Almost all the 103,000 miles of public footpath and bridleway in England and Wales were formed over the centuries by the tramp of people—and their animals—taking the shortest or easiest way to work, to church, to market or the pub.

All public footpaths in England and Wales are marked in red on the 1:50,000 Ordnance Survey maps of England and Wales, and since 1968 Parliament has required county councils to signpost them where they leave a metalled road. In Scotland there is no such requirement because the law on trespass and rights of way is different, but in practice footpaths are often open to walkers. Nevertheless it is wise and courteous to ask permission if you want to tramp across a moor or mountain during the grouse-shooting or deer-stalking seasons.

A stile on the Offa's Dyke long-distance footpath near Pandy

Many farmers plough up public footpaths when they cut diagonally across fields, particularly when they are very rarely used. To re-route them involves a lengthy legal procedure, so you may find your path vanishing in a field of corn. You then have the right to follow the line of the footpath even if it means trampling the corn. However, farmers too can suffer when people picnic in what looks like nice long grass and thereby spoil a crop of hay, or let their dogs run loose to frighten and often injure livestock.

Not all public footpaths are old. Since 1965, when the 250-mile Pennine Way along the spine of England was opened, many more long-distance walks have been carefully planned by the Countryside Commissions for England and Wales and for Scotland and subsequently opened to the public. Marked by discreet arrows, or small yellow thistles in Scotland, they include the 80-mile-long South Downs Way, Offa's Dyke Path along the Welsh borders, and the Cleveland Way in Yorkshire.

Hedges

THE history of British hedgerows is long and fascinating. It is probable that the earliest hedges were linear boundaries of stones, earth or brushwood set down to mark the edges of farms and villages. 'Dead' hedges – stockproof erections of thorny and bushy branches, or pliable wands woven together like loose hurdles – may have been the most common hedges until early medieval times. It is not known for certain when the first living hedges were created, but records have been found showing that many were in existence before the Norman Conquest.

From earliest times hawthorn, being easy to propagate and providing an almost impenetrable thorny barrrier when grown, was the most popular hedging shrub. When the open-field system of agriculture, where huge fields were farmed communally, was superseded by other methods, thousands of miles of hawthorn hedges were planted.

Enclosure of the open fields began as long ago as the mid 15th century, but reached peaks during the late 18th and early 19th centuries. Nearly all of England, except the counties of the south-west, the south-east and the Welsh Marches, was affected by the enclosures of the Georgian period.

Today's hedges

Living hedges require a large amount of labour if they are to remain neat and stock-proof. They also take up considerable areas of good agricultural land. Both these factors have contributed to the loss of hedgerows throughout Britain since World War II. Maintaining a hedge in the traditional way – by 'laying' it – is an expensive undertaking that most modern farmers cannot afford and see no point in. Fences and wire are cheaper to erect and to maintain, and suit some farming methods much better than hedges. In parts of East Anglia, where only arable crops are grown and where huge machines cultivate the ground and harvest the grain, virtually all the hedges have been removed, sometimes leading to loss of soil through wind erosion. Where hedges do remain they are often cut by mechanical flail mowers. While these machines do a very quick job, they leave the hedges looking mangled and bald, and such hedges do not provide the thick cover and luxuriant growth which attracts many kinds of wildlife.

Hedges are still maintained in traditional ways in areas where stockbreeding is paramount, and here beautifully-kept hedges can be found. The best places to see these are along the Welsh borders and in parts of the West Country. Hedges are also used to protect certain crops of flowers, fruit and vegetables in some parts of the country. In recent years the value of hedges as wildlife reserves and as living historical documents has become appreciated, and great efforts are now often made to preserve the most important of them. It is along the hedgerows, whether they be species-rich boundaries perhaps more than a thousand years old or lines of hawthorn planted in the 18th century, that Britain's tremendous variety of wildlife is most likely to be seen.

Key
1 Magpie
2 Bullfinch
3 Sycamore
4 Dog rose (*June–July*)
5 Green-veined white butterfly (*on wing April–June and August–September*)
6 Whitethroat (*summer visitor*)
7 Hawthorn
8 Red campion (*April–August*)
9 Elm
10 Jack-by-the-hedge (*also known as garlic mustard; April–June*)
11 Goldfinch
12 Field mouse
13 Cleavers (*also known as goosegrass; May–August*)
14 False oat grass
15 Lords and ladies (*also known as cuckoo pint; April–June*)
16 Weasel
17 Bank vole
18 Herb robert (*May–October*)
19 Dark bush cricket (*adults active August–November*)
20 Common field thistle (*July–September*)
21 Wolf-spider
22 Hoverfly
23 Annual meadow grass
24 Pigmy shrew
25 Buff-tailed bumble bee
26 Common fumitory (*April–October*)
27 Stoat
28 Magpie
29 Cardinal beetle
30 Soldier beetle
31 Cocksfoot grass
32 Cow parsley (*April–June*)
33 Hogweed (*April–October*)
34 Rosebay willow-herb (*July–September*)
35 Old man's beard (*also known as traveller's joy; July–August*)
36 White bryony (*May–July*)
37 Blackthorn

The plants and animals are not drawn to scale. Plants are in flower during the months shown in brackets.

Walls and Boundaries

Segestria florentina, a spider often found lurking in walls

Zebra spiders are often found on sunny walls. These handsome little creatures catch their prey not by snaring it in webs but by stalking it and then pouncing.

MEN have used walls for thousands of years, not only for buildings, but also as boundaries to fields and farms. In those areas of the country where stone is plentiful, it is the obvious material for field walls, especially since stones had to be cleared from the fields in any case to make cultivation possible.

West Country walls and banks

In some areas boundaries are wall-like barriers of earth or stone rather than lines of trees and shrubs. In the West Country these are often large embankments of earth and stone, with shrubs and trees growing on top, and often up the sides as well. These great barriers were erected as stock-proof boundaries, but they serve an additional function as wind-breaks and shelters. This is especially noticeable on Dartmoor and Exmoor, where the winters can be very severe; here the banks, often more than seven feet high, protect both man and beast from gales and blizzards. Such walls are often exceptionally rich in wildlife, with a profusion of flowers like bluebells, primroses, herb robert, foxglove and red campion growing on them. The shady sides of such walls are often covered in a variety of ferns.

Insects abound in the countless nooks and crannies, as do voles and mice. Stoats and weasels hunt in them for small mammals, and badgers are frequent visitors in search of worms, insects and wasp nests.

On Exmoor many of the earthen boundaries are crowned by beech hedges. These are the field and farm boundaries created by one family, the Knights, during the 19th century. Before that time Exmoor was a wilderness of rough grazing for sheep, but between 1840 and 1850 John Knight and his son Frederick carved half a dozen farms out of the moorland. In all, the Knights enclosed, and created farms on, 15,000 acres of the lovely Exmoor uplands

Some of Dartmoor's stern granite walls are survivors of fields and farms created thousands of years ago. Such walls on bleak upland slopes often enclose tiny fields usually known as 'Celtic fields'. This term is thoroughly misleading, since it is now known that a good many of these fields were ploughed and hedged with walls anything up to 5,000 years ago by the earliest farmers. Ancient fields and walls like these can be traced in many upland areas. They were undoubtedly far more widespread once, but they now only survive in areas where subsequent activities have not destroyed them.

Enclosing the uplands

Throughout the Middle Ages and well into the 16th century vast areas of England were given over to sheep walks. The Cotswolds and the Pennine Chain were open, grassy areas on which sheep, whose wool made England one of Europe's richest countries, wandered at will. Stone walls probably served as 'ranch' boundaries on these immense pastures from very early times, but the majority of the walls that march up hill and down dale for mile after mile in the Cotswolds, Pennines and Lake District were erected in the 18th and 19th centuries during the periods of the Parliamentary enclosures.

Types of wall

Tremendous skill was necessary to build the drystone walls, for they needed to be both stock-proof and weather-proof. Different kinds of stone required different building methods, so a diversity of techniques developed throughout the country. In the Cotswolds the oolitic limestone was easily broken to convenient sizes, but great care was needed to keep rainwater from seeping into the heart of the wall, which would eventually cause its collapse. Even so, a skilled waller could work at great speed, his practised eye always able to pick the right stone for the job. In parts of north Wales the huge boulders of ancient rock are almost impossible to break, so walls were built of complete rocks, the largest at the bottom. Such walls often needed to be very wide at the base to remain stable. In other parts of north Wales both walls and living hedges are replaced by fences of slate; often these are simply huge slabs stuck into the ground next to each other. Many of the Lake District pastures were once littered with millions of tons of stones. These are now incorporated into great walls, but there was too much stone even for all the walls, and in places piles, or islands, of neatly stacked stones linked by walls dot the Lakeland landscapes.

The plants of walls

Lime mortar was used until recently to bind walls of both stone and brick, and since it is rich in calcium it is very attractive to many plants. As the mortar slowly crumbles with age such plants are able to find a roothold in the tiny fissures and crevices that develop. Common among these are stonecrop and wall rocket. One of the most lovely of wall plants is red valerian, introduced from the Mediterranean as a garden plant in the 16th century, but now found growing wild in many areas. Another introduced plant that has long been established in the wild is the aptly-named wallflower.

Lichens and mosses can be found on walls of all sorts in unpolluted areas; while certain ferns – notably hart's tongue – are tough enough to withstand growing on sooty chimney stacks.

Red valerian growing on the walls of the ruined Bishop's Palace at St David's in south Wales

A drystone wall close to Borgue, a tiny village near Kircudbright. Such walls are called 'dykes' in Scotland

The Farming Landscape Today

Something like 80% of the British countryside is farmland of one sort or another, which means that there are very few truly wild places left. Even remote Scottish hillsides are grazed by sheep. And over the last 30 years there have been tremendous changes in agriculture which have affected the traditional patchwork of the countryside. Yet the farming landscape remains fascinatingly diverse, still essentially linked to the ancient elements of the weather and the land itself.

Stubble burning in the wheat fields of East Anglia

Weeds
Selective herbicides and cleaner seed corn have reduced the abundance and diversity of weeds once commonly seen in Britain's cornfields. The rosy purple corncockle, scarlet poppy and pheasant's eye are rarities now in sprayed fields of immaculate wheat or barley. Some manage to retain a hold, like yellow charlock, one of the most persistent and always regarded as a pest; or common ragwort, whose leaves are poisonous to livestock. Ironically, some plants regarded as weeds were once grown for food. These include sorrel, which was a favourite vegetable in Tudor times, and fat hen, whose juicy green leaves taste like spinach. Both fat hen and corn spurrey, a tangling little white-flowered plant known as 'pickpurse' in some areas because of its damaging effect on grain yields, were cultivated for food at least 2,000 years ago.

The diversity of soil

It is much wetter in the west of Britain than in the east, and there is a rapid drop in temperature as you go north or climb even a few hundred feet. Within a single county there are often enormous differences in the configuration of the land, so that in Worcestershire it is possible to travel from the neat orchards of the Vale of Evesham to the buzzard-circled heights of the Malvern Hills, or in Devon from lush wooded combes to the treeless tors of Dartmoor. Soils can even change within a field. Agricultural land is classified according to its fertility, from Grade 1 to Grade 5, and it varies throughout the country.

All these factors fundamentally affect the farming landscape. In the south-western lowlands of both England and Scotland fields tend to be small and hedged because dairy cows thrive on their rich grass, and cows need shelter, changes of pasture and hay or silage in winter. On the drier, flat lands of East Anglia corn pays better, and because giant combine harvesters need room to manoeuvre, there are great treeless expanses of wheat and barley stretching to the horizon. On the thin, stony soils of the Welsh, Scottish and English northern hills, sheep and hardy beef cattle do best, and stone walls mark their fields and folds. Down on the black peat fens of Cambridgeshire or the fertile alluvial loams of river valleys, soft fruit and vegetables are grown on what are often the finest and most productive Grade I soils. Other factors have affected

the look of the farming landscape in recent years. Dutch elm disease has now killed about 15 million English elms which were once so much part of the landscape. Government grants and aid from the European Economic Community encourage farmers to reclaim uncultivated areas which would otherwise remain as natural habitats for wildlife, by draining, ploughing and reseeding.

Changes in farming practice

Modern technology plays a subtler role. Farmers today use 20 times as much artificial fertilizer as they did 30 years ago, and so wheat is grown every year in the same field instead of being rotated with grazing or other crops. Grass meadows are often much greener and more uniform than they used to be, because the old mixtures of grasses cannot compete with new rye grass strains when fertilized with nitrogen. Such grass is often grown for silage instead of hay, which means it can be cut both earlier and more frequently in the year. It is not left to dry but put straight into tall silos, clamps or black polythene bags, its great advantage being that the farmer does not have 'to make hay while the sun shines'.

Herbicides have almost eradicated many weeds once common in cornfields, among them sorrel, corncockles and the scarlet poppy – although poppy seeds can last a hundred years and poppies will always reappear somewhere, like many other wild plants. In autumn fields looking quite brown and dead can be seen: these will not be ploughed, but direct-drilled, the old crop killed off with a total herbicide and the new seed sown straight into the ground. Or the stubble fields will be burned, because much of the straw from wheat and barley is no longer needed as bedding for livestock.

New strains of crops are always being developed, and what looks like old-fashioned mustard is likely to be the vivid yellow of oilseed rape in bloom in spring. Heavy cream-coloured Charolais cattle are one of the breeds recently introduced from France, and in the south of England maize or even commercial vineyards may be seen.

Although only 3% of people now live on the land, Britain is 70% self-sufficient in temperate foodstuffs. Small farms have been amalgamated, the old landlord and tenant system has declined and many arable areas are owned by large financial institutions. It often makes the landscape look rather empty and bland.

However, a good many farmers still own the land they farm and have a deep affection for it, and combine efficient food production with the maintenance of a traditional mixed pattern of farming: a dairy herd, young beef cattle, some corn, silage or hay and often a small flock of sheep. Many enjoy hunting and shooting and look after woodland and hedgerows which are good for all wildlife as well as foxes and pheasants. Farming has changed least of all in the upland areas. Sturdy stone houses crouch low against the wind, with sheepfolds close to home and collies kenneled by the back door, watching the distant sheep.

On the downs near Alfriston, Sussex. Although the Romans cultivated parts of the downs, it was not until the 20th century that farmers began to turn many of the downland sheep walks into huge arable fields

Game farming

Few people are surprised to see a pheasant strutting along the roadside, although the male, with his sweeping tail and iridescent plumage, is a particularly exotic-looking bird. Probably introduced from Asia as a domestic fowl by the Romans, pheasants have been reared for shooting since the 18th century. Many hedgerows, copses and woodlands are conserved for the sport and field corners are often planted with kale, maize or sunflowers for winter feed.

The grey partridge is found throughout much of Britain

The grey native partridge is a quiet, rather dumpy little bird, but it is much less common than the pheasant because its habitat of open fields and hedgerows has been badly affected by modern farming techniques which burn stubble after harvest and make liberal use of pesticides. The red-legged partridge, which was introduced from France in the 18th century, is increasingly being both artificially reared and naturally encouraged. Red-legged partridges can often be seen in coveys of up to a hundred on open land.

Foxhunting

Foxes were once regarded as vermin, to be trapped and killed in their earths. The nobler quarries were the deer and the hare. But as the land was increasingly enclosed in the 18th century and the deer retreated to wilder fastnesses, foxhunting became a fashionable sport. It was realized that foxes ran straight and swift across country, and jumping hedges added to the thrill of the chase. By the end of the 18th century great hunts like the Quorn and the Belvoir were established. All over the country foxhunting landowners planted new coverts and woods to encourage the fox – a legacy which greatly enriched the landscape. Today foxhunting still flourishes, and it is undoubtedly true that much of Britain's remaining woodland would be viewed as a useless luxury and felled if foxhunting were to be banned.

Around the Farm

A Shropshire farmhouse, surrounded by its homely muddle of buildings from many periods

Livestock breeds

The most common breed of cattle in Britain is the black and white Friesian dairy cow, although the dark red and white Ayrshire still predominates in Scotland. Other common breeds include the widespread white-faced Hereford and black Aberdeen Angus among the traditional beef breeds, and the elegant Jerseys and Guernseys with their rich Channel Islands milk. More recent are breeds introduced from the Continent, like the Charolais, Simmental and Holstein. Most farmers now employ artificial insemination to produce calves, and bulls are rare on farms, though beef cattle on open pasture are still likely to be served by bulls.

Pigs, too, are often bred by artificial insemination. The Large White is the most popular of the nine main British breeds, although many pigs are now bred by crossing traditional breeds to produce vigorous hybrid strains.

With the highest density of sheep to the square mile of any country except New Zealand, Britain has more than 40 different breeds. Most numerous are the hill sheep like the Cheviot, Welsh Mountain and Blackface, which live wild in their own territories throughout the year.

Many old breeds are now being revived, partly because their qualities of disease resistance and hardiness may be useful if present breeds suffer from too much emphasis on other characteristics.

THE FARMHOUSE is a vital component of the British countryside. It might be half-timbered black-and-white in the Midlands or East Anglia, thatched in Devon, or low and whitewashed in Scotland. In the north of England and in the Welsh hills, farmhouses are of sturdy grey rubble stone, slate or granite, and in Suffolk and Essex they are often limewashed, their plaster pargeted in intricate patterns. Weatherboarded and half-tiled houses in Kent and Sussex are frequently topped by turreted oasthouses for drying hops, as are many of the farmhouses in Herefordshire and Worcestershire. Farmhouses reflect the availability of local building materials and styles, and in most districts brick houses are common, including elegantly proportioned Georgian farmhouses, workers' cottages and monumental Victorian 'model' farms complete with dovecoted barns.

There are few modern farmhouses. Many date back to the great age of rural rebuilding in the late 16th and early 17th centuries. Many more have become ordinary private dwellings as their land has been sold off and amalgamated with neighbouring farms. But you can always tell a working farmhouse. Beyond its garden gate is the farmyard, often muddy or hay-strewn, surrounded by barns, cowsheds, machinery stores, manure heaps and railed yards for cattle.

Farm buildings

Because they are busy workplaces farms rarely look tidy to an outsider. Farmers do not pay rates on their farm buildings and therefore often put up new ones without knocking the old ones down. There is always a need for storage. Farms usually have a conglomeration of buildings, ranging from lopsided old wooden granaries sitting on staddle stones (to keep them clear of rats) to the tall skeletal Dutch barns made of steel and corrugated iron, which are really just a development of a thatched haystack open to the air on all sides. Today, with hay declining in importance as winter feed, the Dutch barn is giving way to aluminium silos in which grass is cut and fermented as silage. More recently, silage clamps have become very common. Covered with black polythene and weighted down with old rubber tyres, they provide a permanent source

of food at which the cattle can munch away as they please. The latest development is to put the silage into giant polythene bags out in the fields where it is cut, and where it will later be fed to livestock without having to transport it back to the farm. Consequently many Dutch barns now house bags of fertilizer and machinery instead of sweet-smelling bales, although hay is still made on many farms, particularly in the hills, usually in late June.

Farm animals

Although fewer hens are seen scratching about in farmyards today, there are often more animals actually on the farm than there used to be. Dairy herds tend to be larger, many of up to a hundred cows housed in vast covered yards during the winter. To speed the process by which 30 million pints of milk a day arrive on British doorsteps, milking 'parlours' are frequently highly automated. Rotary and herringbone designs enable one man to milk five cows at a time within ten minutes. Their feed may be dispensed by a computer which can calculate precisely how much each cow requires according to the stage of her lactation. Bulk milk tanks in the dairy keep the milk cool until it is collected for national distribution by the blue tankers of the Milk Marketing Board, or, less commonly, processed and sold on the farm itself.

Over 90% of the eggs bought in Britain are produced from hens in battery cages. Like pigs, often similarly kept, they live out their brief lives in a carefully controlled and enclosed environment. But pigs are still seen outside in the fields, with small corrugated iron shelters known as 'arcs' provided for each breeding sow. Deep litter housing for hens, a fairly traditional practice, is often continued. The hens are kept in sheds with straw bedding, having a considerable degree of freedom, and sometimes access to outside runs.

Sheep do not thrive in enclosed conditions, and are only brought into the farmyard itself on rare occasions, sometimes for lambing or routine operations like dipping or shearing. However, on an increasing number of farms, sheep are overwintered in covered sheep yards. This minimizes labour, and prevents the sheep damaging heavy land by trampling it.

Top: harvesting wheat in Humberside
Above: an ultra-modern four-wheel drive tractor

From horses to helicopters
Heavy horses have made something of a comeback on farms in recent years, particularly on smaller farms and where compaction of certain soils by heavy vehicles can be a problem. Nevertheless since Henry Ford developed the tractor early in this century there have been tremendous advances in agricultural machinery. On almost every farm there is a considerable range of equipment: harrows, cultivators, seed drills, and forage harvesters or hay mowers. On arable farms combine harvesters lumber across the ripe corn fields in late summer, and throughout the year boom spreaders, spinners and even crop-spraying aircraft dispense fertilizers, pesticides, fungicides and herbicides on the crops. Diesel oil tanks and well-equipped workshops are as vital as ploughs and barns on almost every farm today, and the farmworker has to be a skilled technician.

Below: heavy horses are seen pulling a harrow, a device used after ploughing to reduce the soil to a fine tilth

Yesterday's Farm

The hurdle-maker
In the picture above a hurdle-maker is splitting a rod. He is using a billhook to do the actual splitting, and keeps the ends apart with his arm, which is protected by the uppers of an old boot. The split rods were woven in and out of stout upright poles that were fixed into a frame at ground level. When the weaving was complete the hurdle was lifted clear of the frame. Such hurdles were used to form protective shelters for livestock, and were also frequently used as a kind of harrow, being drawn across the soil to produce a tilth. Hurdles made from willow wood were used until the 19th century.

IN LESS than 60 years technology has transformed Britain's farms, but reminders of the old farming way of life remain.

Many of the tools and machines used on yesterday's farm can still be found. They may lie rotting and forgotten in a field, or they may be lovingly preserved and used as the centrepiece in a pub or museum display. Rusty hand tools, their function no longer clear, occasionally turn up in dark corners of garden sheds. A very few are still in use today. One of the most astonishing things about these tools, many of which were in everyday use until little more than a century ago, is their variety. For example, there were more than half-a-dozen pronged tools specially designed for pulling up different kinds of deep-rooted weeds. One tool still widely used is the billhook, but it is not commonly known that in the 19th century, when almost every good blacksmith made hooks to his own design, there were scores of different hooks.

Changing ways
Until the 1920s an average-sized farm needed several wagons and carts, a large number of ploughs, and hundreds of smaller but equally essential machines and tools. These included turnip crushers, barrows, sieves, rakes, knives and shears. Several teams of horses were needed to pull the machines and vehicles, and large numbers of labourers were essential to the smooth running of the farm. Nowadays, huge tractors, multi-furrow reversible ploughs and harvesters accomplish in a day what once took weeks, and the average workforce has been reduced to the farmer himself and one labourer.

Above: threshing corn in Westmorland. Unthreshed corn is being fed into the top of the threshing machine, and the grain is being collected in sacks at the side of the machine while straw is ejected at the end

Left: reaping a barley crop with scythes

Horsedrawn vehicles

Carts and wagons were an essential part of every farm from prehistoric times until the advent of tractors and trailers. Carts changed very little in shape and construction during that long period. Their simple construction of a single axle, two wheels and a pair of shafts to enclose the horse needed very little modification to suit a variety of needs. Farm carts were used primarily to carry dung – a dense and heavy load that required a solid base and strong sides. Dung carts were arranged so that the body could be tipped backwards with the horse still in harness. It would have been a tedious task to release the horse each time the cart was tipped, especially on days when the cart was in use from dawn till dusk.

Wagons have a more complex history, and several variations arose on the basic construction of two axles – the front one pivoted to enable the vehicle to turn – linked by a pole. In Victorian times, partly as a result of mass production, other frameworks began to appear. There were two basic wagon types in England until the 19th century – box wagons and hoop-raved wagons. Box wagons, although capable of variation, were always basically boxes, and hoop raved wagons had their bodywork arched above the rear wheel, with the top rave, or rail, curved in a characteristic manner. Many regional variations on these basic types were developed over the centuries. As a result of mass production wagon construction was simplified and became less pleasing in appearance, but the later boat and barge wagons still retained much of the grace of their predecessors.

The shepherd

For centuries the shepherd was one of the country's most important agricultural workers. He spent most of his time on the sheepwalks with only the sheep for company, and was in many ways the most independent of rural labourers. His life was usually very hard, and often shepherds became crippled with rheumatism and arthritis after years spent in the open in every kind of weather. Many lived for the greater part of the year in rough shelters built into the hillsides, but some improvements came in the 19th century, when cabins on wheels were introduced. The shepherd's lonely vigil often included miles of fruitless searching for lost sheep and even becoming surrogate mother to orphaned lambs.

The Village

Snowshill, a Cotswold village built almost entirely of the lovely local stone. The church was rebuilt in the same material in 1864

Mills and millers

A method of grinding corn has been vital to man ever since he harvested the first meagre crop of grain, and the earliest form of mill is the quern, composed of two grindstones of which one was turned by hand. In the 1st century the Greeks invented the watermill, subsequently introduced to Britain by the Romans and developed by the Anglo-Saxons. Windmills were probably brought from the Middle East by returning Crusaders in the 12th century. Both powered the great grindstones and were to become central features of village life, since everyone either took corn to them for grinding, or bought flour from the miller who owned them. Most mills stopped working before, or shortly after, World War II. But some are grinding corn again in response to a revival of interest in stoneground flour.

Millers were once notorious figures. They were supposed to exact a small percentage of the flour they ground as a toll, but were frequently prosecuted for taking more. It was once said that 'hair grows in the palm of an honest miller'.

SOMEHOW, in a fast-changing world, the village seems to remain much as it always was. It has had to adjust, of course: to the internal combustion engine, to the decline in rural employment, to commuters and county planning officers. But then it has never been static. Ever since the Anglo-Saxons sailed up the rivers of England to settle in pleasant lowland valleys, the village has been the organic nucleus of a community. Every village is different: every village shares the same essential elements, like the parish church, the pub, the post office, the Women's Institute and the darts team – and a strong sense of its own identity.

Early settlements

The Celts of the Iron Age were not a peaceful pastoral people, and favoured hilltop forts which could be defended against invaders or belligerent neighbours. The Romans who succeeded them belonged to an essentially urban society, and towns were vital to their administration of this damp northern province. But the Anglo-Saxons, Jutes and Danes let the Roman towns crumble, while with their ploughs and great hand-axes they cleared the land for their farms. Many place names echo the early consolidation of such small communities in which particular families predominated, like Hullavington in Wiltshire, founded by Hunlaf's people.

When Christianity re-established itself in the 7th century, churches became focal points for society. Many of our present parish churches were built on the sites of those originally built to serve a lord's estate, and some still stand, like St Peter-ad-Murum in Essex or St Lawrence in Bradford-on-Avon, Wiltshire. It was around the church and the lord's hall that settlements formed, their boundaries often marked by living fences of quickthorn which account for a proportion of our hedgerows today.

In 1066 the Normans introduced a feudal system, a vigorous church, an influx of new monastic foundations which opened up remote parts of the countryside – and the rabbit, bred in warrens, or 'conygers', for food. In the same way pigeons were fattened in dovecotes, swans in swanneries, deer in parks and carp in fishponds. Manors, monasteries, home farms and hunting forests governed the growth of villages. Water and windmills were important: 5,624 watermills for grinding corn were recorded in the Domesday Book of 1086. The peasants, or villeins, served their manorial lord before they attended to their own field strips. Their straying animals ended up in the village pound.

During mediaeval times villages continued to develop according to local needs. In the hills of Scotland and Wales there were fewer villages and more isolated hamlets and farmsteads, whose people moved up from the sheltered valleys in summer to shielings or the Welsh hafods for grazing cattle and sheep. Along West Country rivers massive weirs were built for the fulling mills which beat woollen weave into heavy broadcloth. On the Norfolk coast, villages like Cley-next-the-Sea, now far from the sea on its silted marshes, became major ports, distinguished by fine churches.

Deserted villages

Over the centuries more than 2,000 villages were deserted. Many of these are identifiable today by humps and depressions in unploughed fields, by solitary churches, or from the air by uneven patterns of growth in crops. Grain will be stunted where it grows on old foundations, but flourishes over a trench or the nitrogenous waste of ancient rubbish tips. The Normans had eradicated some villages to make way for royal hunting areas like the New Forest, or for sheep and the privacy of monks like those of Revesby Abbey in Lincolnshire. Coastal erosion destroyed others. Then in the 14th century the Black Death killed more than half the people in England; there were also subsequent ecclesiastical manoeuvres between rival dioceses which shifted the remaining population from one parish to another. Sometimes people simply decided that their village was too wet and cold for comfort, as probably they did at Cold Weston in Shropshire. A few landowners decided to improve their surroundings by completely rebuilding villages, as happened at Milton Abbas in Dorset and Blanchland in Northumberland at the turn of the 18th century: the archetypal English village, with its thatch and village green, was already recognized as having its own particular charm.

Cottages at Aringour, a port on the island of Coll in the Inner Hebrides where community living still retains many traditional aspects

Watermills and windmills
Watermills were a source of power in many developing industries and remained so until they were supplanted by steam at the end of the 18th century. Several survive today, and at Priston village in Somerset a watermill still grinds corn just as it did when recorded in the Domesday Book of 1086. Its flour produces excellent wholemeal bread.

Priston watermill

Windmills were made in three different types. The earliest was the post-mill, in which the whole body of the mill revolves around a central oak post. The oldest surviving today, built in 1665, is at Outwood in Surrey. Later came the tower and smock mills, on which only the sails move: the fixed bodies are of brick, stone, or the weatherboarding which must have reminded someone of a countryman's smock. The sails were originally made of canvas laced on wooden latticework, then of hinged shutters. A windmill is still a dramatic sight and one of the finest is the Union Mill, a smock mill, at Cranbrook in Kent.

The Village

Set among the hills of the West Riding of Yorkshire, Todmorden grew from an isolated village during the industrial expansion of the 19th century

A wealth of villages

The 18th century was a time of expansion and prosperity in many fields, not least in agriculture and rural industries, and villages were expanding too. There were no planners, and architects designed only great houses: if a farmer, a mill owner, a shopkeeper or a wheelwright wanted a new house, he went to the local builder and chose one from a book of patterns, which was built for him in whatever local material might be available. The result was that although no two houses were ever exactly the same, because even two of the same basic pattern would have different embellishments, they did share a harmony of style and materials. So there are narrow, pink and grey villages in the Mendips, rosy brick and half-tiled villages in Sussex, flint in East Anglia; villages of tucked-in grey stone in the Yorkshire Dales, meandering thatched villages in Dorset and Devon, white weatherboarded villages in Kent and golden limestone villages in the Cotswolds. Every district varies, every arrangement of houses and cottages is unique, whether around a slow stream, a market square or a village green.

The industrial countryside

With the Industrial Revolution, which began in the 18th century, a new kind of village began to appear, specifically built to provide housing for workers in the iron, coal, textile and manufacturing industries. Bleak but close-knit terraces were cobbled together on the once-green hillsides from Yorkshire to South Wales, Lancashire to the Mendips. Working men's clubs and Methodist chapels were their social centres, not manor houses and mediaeval parish churches.

Yet in many ways these industrial villages were much closer to their existing rural counterparts than later and often sentimentalized pictures of village life might suggest. The Industrial Revolution was a gradual process, and until the end of the 19th century the countryside was by no means purely agricultural. Every kind of trade and manufacture flourished wherever local materials and demand allowed. Among the cornfields and cows were mining – copper, tin and lead – smelting, brick-making, quarrying, and every aspect of timber production. The processes of cloth-making, dyeing and fulling, like those which accompanied local animal slaughter – glue-making, tanning and fertilizer production – were common, and so were the smells and pollution which went with them. Quite apart from local services such as saddlery and blacksmithing, many rural outworkers were employed in their own homes, making ribbons, finishing garments, grinding steel for the cutlery industry. Agriculture itself demanded a whole range of skills. And whether the villagers worked in a cotton mill, a fishing boat, down the mine or on the farm, they went early, returned late, and earned very little for their labour. What they did possess was a very strong sense of community, and a knowledge of husbandry and the countryside which was their particular inheritance. Each village could be self-contained, and even impoverished cottagers tried to grow some vegetables and keep a few chickens and perhaps a pig.

Churchyards

In many villages the oldest building is the parish church. One of the most characteristic features of the British landscape is a sturdy tower on the skyline, its bells a summons to everyone around. And almost every church has its churchyard, usually a consecrated burial ground in which no parishioner, no matter who or what his position in life, can be denied interment after death.

There are about a hundred carefully clipped yew trees in the churchyard at Painswick

The churchyard is usually owned jointly by the parson and the parochial church council, who can regulate, although they do not own, the memorial stones placed on the graves. In the past, although it was against church law, many country vicars grazed their cattle and sheep in the churchyards, so that the graves had to be fenced with osiers or brambles. Today sheep still graze some churchyards to keep the grass down, but permission is required.

Yew trees often grow in churchyards, and to a great age: the remains of the Fortingall yew in a churchyard on Tayside in Scotland once measured 50 feet round and could be nearly 2,000 years old. Explanations for their abundance in churchyards are many and varied. Some say they date from pagan times, or that they were planted to provide wood for the longbowmen of England and had to be kept in churchyards because their foliage is poisonous to cattle and sheep – birds, however, eat the harmless fleshy part of the berry and pass the seed unharmed.

The gentry were normally commemorated within the church, but from the middle of the 17th century prosperous farmers and craftsmen could afford gravestones in the churchyard. Not only do many of them paradoxically bring the past vividly alive by their inscriptions, often tragic in their indication of early death, but provide fascinating hosts for lichens which flourish best in untouched places and in unpolluted air.

Changing times and changing ways

Since the bustling heyday of the village in the 19th century there has been a steady and often rapid decline in rural populations. The trend has been somewhat reversed over the past 20 years as more and more people have moved out of the cities, but they have affected chiefly those villages with easy access to towns. Nor have they replaced the original inhabitants, but rather introduced a new and sometimes disturbing element. Some village cottages have become second homes whose owners take no part in village life save to appear at weekends and patronize their rustic neighbours. Others, retiring to the country for its picturesque unspoiled charm, have resisted attempts to bring new small industries or trades to the village, thereby preventing the chances of any future employment for the young people of the area.

Yet the village, as ever, adapts. Uneasy as the mix between the old and new breeds of countrydweller may be, the villager who happens to commute to work 30 miles away each day often takes a great pride in his village. He may bring a new enthusiasm to village life, perhaps joining the horticultural association or the cricket team; his wife may play a valuable role in the Women's Institute or local playgroup, and their children by their very presence keep the village school – and to some degree the church – alive. It was this new breed of villager who pursued the campaign for real ale in pubs, and who often revived an interest in local history. Self-sufficiency may prompt amusement among old inhabitants of a village, but nevertheless they like to see hens scratching in an orchard again, and there is a new fascination with cottage garden plants. Where old and new villagers can appreciate each other's value, when the urban country-dweller can understand the reticent pride of the farmer and farmworker, the village thrives as perhaps it never did when people had no choice but to live within its confines.

Village shops sold a vast array of goods: from clothes to sweets and from galvanized buckets to coal

Village tradesmen
Tradesmen fulfilled an essential role in communities that were virtually self-supporting. Among the most respected were blacksmiths, whose forges were often meeting places where village politics and local scandals were discussed. Blacksmiths used their hearths and anvils not only to shoe horses but to mend anything from a plough to a bicycle, while frequently producing very fine wrought ironwork.

Other skilled village tradesmen included wheelwrights, saddlers, thatchers, tilers, stonemasons and brewers. Up on the hill there would be hurdle-makers, cutting the chestnut, ash and hazel for sheep pens and cattle yards, and in the woods charcoal burners carefully cut and charred the timber.

MUCH has changed in the village since the end of World War II, that watershed of traditional and modern in the countryside. Yet a great deal remains of the immediate past. There is a vivid photographic record of the early years of this century, and many country people, transported 50 years forward from Victorian times to the 1930s, would have found village life much the same. Old people can talk of how things used to be, and like to do so. And there are written accounts, notably Flora Thompson's *Lark Rise to Candleford*, which describe in loving detail the life of yesterday's village.

Perhaps the most fundamental difference between a village today and some 60 years ago is that its population, unless artificially enlarged by suburbia or by becoming an urban overspill new town, would then have been much greater. Everybody, rich or poor, tended to have big families, and there was almost always sufficient employment to keep children within the district. Wealthy landowners lived in surrounding country houses and employed enormous numbers of indoor servants and estate workers, gardeners, gamekeepers and farm labourers. Although mechanization came early to farms it was still a supplement to men and horses – in 1910 there were 1,137,000 heavy horses working on the land, probably more than ever before or since.

A quiet corner of yesterday's village

Recipes

Most village housewives have always prided themselves on their shining shelves of home-made preserves, pickles and jams. Competition at produce shows is keen, and in the middle of winter nothing tastes of summer quite so much as home-made jam in a cotton-bonneted jar. Many countrywomen also find uses for the free flowers and fruits they can gather along their own hedgerows, in the fields and even on the seashore. Not all old recipes and remedies are as good as they sound, but many are worth trying.

The elder tree is one of the most common in the countryside and its creamy curds of blossom in early summer make a delicate sparkling wine. A muslin bag of dried elderflowers, steeped in the bath, is said to soften the skin and calm the nerves. Stress, it seems, is no new problem! Chamomile's white daisies, infused into tea, have always been recommended as a soothing drink. They also bring out the highlights in blonde hair when used as a final rinse. Dandelions make a good pungent wine, especially if root ginger is included.

Most fruits produce good wine, elderberries being particularly suitable. Rose hips are perhaps best used for rose hip syrup, simply made with water and honey: the resulting sweet syrup can be diluted to make a drink rich in Vitamin C, or poured over ice cream. Rowanberries make a very fine bittersweet jelly for serving with pork or game.

Mushrooms have always been gathered from cattle pastures in autumn – the best time is very early in the morning. Puffballs, like small moons suddenly appearing in orchards and meadows, are delicious sliced and fried with bacon and a little garlic. Good with bacon, too, is laverbread, made from seaweed and particularly popular in Wales.

Shops

Very few people owned cars in yesterday's village, and so shops were important. Even the wealthier middle classes used the village for most of their shopping. In a large community there might be room for a bakery, a butcher, an ironmongery and a grocer's shop, usually a post office and a draper's. In a small village one shop might do for almost everything – and anything – that people could possibly want: a length of cotton, a pound of China tea, a wheelbarrow, a cheese, yards of lace, a nutmeg or a remedy for piles. The village shop certainly had a good store of one of the most necessary commodities in a small community – gossip. Usually located at the most central part of the village, the shopkeeper could pass on titbits of information to her customers.

People were not only more numerous, but much less mobile. A country road was seldom a quiet backwater in which a car might occasionally ruffle the cow parsley at 50 miles an hour. There were carts, wagons, people on foot. Even today there are country people who have never travelled farther than 20 miles distant, and who recall a time when passers-by in the village were not usually strangers driving past or tourists admiring the thatch, but regular acquaintances, the men who filled in the holes in the road, farmworkers, coalmen, draymen, and all the other tradesmen operating in a single area. Pubs were really local, not simply known as such by those who might work 50 miles away, with beer and cider barrels in the landlord's front room and pub games like shove ha'penny, cribbage or dominoes.

Leisure and work

As far as entertainment went, people in the village either created it themselves or depended upon a few travelling showmen. There was usually a church social, summer outings, a fête and a flower show, and the fairground would make an annual visit to the green. There were sometimes Penny Readings when visiting entertainers read passages from books or plays in the village schoolroom. There were shooting parties at country houses in the winter, giving local boys a chance to earn some money by beating or picking up the pheasants. Time nevertheless hung heavy for many people, particularly the young, although domestic chores necessarily took much longer: there was always, for women at least, much sewing to be done, the making of jams and pickles, bottling and brewing home made wines, salting beans, curing hams and boiling up the great coppers for doing the washing with mangle and flat-iron to follow.

Everybody knew everybody in the village then, and most people would probably have said that they knew their place and were proud of it. Even to have a place on the bottom rung of the social scale was perhaps better than to have no place at all, and everyone, from the squire to the village simpleton, felt he or she had some value to that small community.

81

Cottage Gardens

ToDAY's cottage gardens, with their wealth of flowers, fruits and vegetables, are the culmination of thousands of years of observation, experiment and careful tending. All cultivated plants are, of course, descended from wild ancestors. The knowledge of which plants were good to eat, or had some beneficial property, as well as of those plants which were poisonous or inedible, was learned slowly over many generations. Most of this knowledge was passed on by word of mouth, but authors of the Classical world, writing over 2,000 years ago, began the long tradition of compiling books about plants and their uses.

The Romans introduced the first formal gardens to Britain, and at the excavated villa at Fishbourne in Sussex, a garden can be seen which is laid out on the original plan and planted with species known to have been cultivated there.

There are few records of medieval gardens; those which do survive describe gardens which were attached to the homes of the rich and powerful, and to monasteries. It was in monastery gardens that many of the medicinal herbs were grown, so that when the monasteries were dissolved in the 1530s, ordinary folk who had previously obtained physic plants from them were obliged to cultivate their own.

Herbs were probably the most important plants in early gardens. Meat was the staple food of all classes, but it was often of poor quality, and frequently eaten when nearly rotten, so a surprising variety of herbs was used to disguise and improve many dishes. Herbs and other plants were also used in every branch of medicine, from removing blemishes to curing serious illnesses.

The majority of country labourers lived in dismal hovels until well into the 16th century (and much, much later in many areas) and such places probably had no gardens attached to them. At best they would have had a yard, or patch of ground in which a few basic vegetables were grown. These would include cabbages, beans and root crops, as well as plants like fat hen and nettles that are regarded as weeds today. Potatoes, the staple crop in many a garden, were not commonly grown in England until late in the 18th century. A pig and a hen or two were kept by those who could afford them.

It was not until the closing decades of the 18th century that cottage gardens of the kind beloved today began to appear in large numbers. At this time some enlightened landlords began to provide better housing for their labourers, and with such accommodation often went a sizeable plot of land. It was also at this time that the gentry began to live in country cottages and started to cultivate their own gardens.

By the mid 19th century there were beautiful cottage gardens throughout the country – and they belonged equally to the working people and to the gentry. Gardens – some small, some large – were created in which vegetables, flowers, herbs, fruit trees and ornamental shrubs grew together in a glorious mixture. Artists and writers recorded, in great detail, the appearance of these gardens. Some of the descriptions and paintings are idealized, but then the conception of a perfect cottage garden is in itself an ideal; one that is somehow peculiarly and charmingly British.

Key

 1 Hollyhock
 2 Scarlet pimpernel
   (*May–September*)
 3 Germander speedwell
   (*March–July*)
 4 Large black slug
 5 Garden slug
 6 Greenfinch
 7 House sparrow (*female*)
 8 Greater plantain
 9 Wallflower
10 Honeysuckle
11 House martin (*summer visitor*)
12 House martin nest
13 Lavender
14 Song thrush
15 House martin
16 Delphinium
17 Stock
18 House sparrow (*male*)
19 Garden snail
20 Woodlice
21 Small tortoiseshell butterfly
   (*on wing June and also
   August–September*)
22 Honesty
23 Lupin
24 Robin
25 Pansy
26 House mouse
27 Groundsel
   (*January–December*)
28 Rosemary
29 Shepherd's purse
   (*January–December*)
30 Daisy (*March–October*)
31 Seven-spot ladybird
32 Garden spider
33 White dead-nettle
   (*March–November*)
**The animals and plants are
not drawn to scale. Plants are
in flower during the months
shown in brackets**

Above: the yellow flower is Oxford ragwort, an introduced plant found only in Oxford until the 19th century, when it began to spread along the railway network

Right: ducks on the village pond at Urchfont, Wiltshire

Roundabouts

The centres of roundabouts, especially the larger ones, can be interesting places to explore. Often the roundabout encircles a patch of countryside that has not been disturbed since it was built. A large, partially completed road junction in Hampshire serves as an example of what can be found. At its centre is a marshy area thick with reeds and willow. Damselflies flit across the water, small birds nest in the willows and other shrubby trees, and kestrels hover above hunting for rodents and other small creatures. On the raised embankments which carry the road surfaces orchids and many other wild flowers grow. Such forgotten corners of the countryside can be found throughout Britain and they are always worth investigation, for although man may find no use for them, wild plants and animals will take advantage of any available undisturbed space.

Ponds

UNTIL the advent of piped water supplies village ponds were often the only source of relatively fresh water in a village and supplied water for drinking, cooking and washing. Horses, of which there were over a million in pre-mechanized Britain, were watered at them, and scolds and other village miscreants were ducked in them. By the first half of this century most were disused and many had become muddy eyesores or dumping grounds for rubbish. Recently, various campaigns, both local and national, have resulted in hundreds of village ponds being cleaned out and tidied up. The banks may be neatly cut, and a local benefactor may have donated a seat or two from which the antics of the ducks and village goings-on may be

watched. Village ponds may be havens for a host of invertebrates, fish, moorhens, coots, the occasional heron, newts and frogs. The loss of wet areas and natural pools through land reclamation and drainage has led to a sharp decline in amphibians in the countryside, and it is possible that their greatest densities may one day be in village ponds and suburban gardens with ponds.

Waste ground

Nearly every village, town and city has patches of waste ground that are either awaiting development or seem simply to have been forgotten. Such places are often used as unofficial rubbish tips or playgrounds, but they can also be unofficial nature reserves.

Plants which like to grow on disturbed ground thrive on them. These include rosebay willowherb, thistles, nettles and poppies. Rosebay willowherb is the food plant of the handsome elephant hawk moth, and nettles are food for the caterpillars of butterflies like the red admiral, comma and tortoiseshell. The flowering heads of thistles attract the adults of these and other butterflies. Poppies once grew in profusion in cornfields throughout the country, but chemical sprays have eradicated them from most fields, and they are now most likely to be seen in large numbers on waste ground. One of the loveliest shrubs found in such places is buddleia, whose flowers attract a host of butterflies.

Birds can find both food and nesting places on waste ground. Robins, past masters at building nests in incongruous places, may build in old kettles, piles of bricks or under the wheel arches of abandoned cars. Goldfinches will feed on the seed heads of thistles, dandelions and other plants, and willow warblers and chiff-chaffs may flit among the willows that quickly colonize open ground. At ground level mice, voles and rats may be found, as well as more unusual creatures such as lizards and slow-worms. Many foxes make their homes amid the rubble and overgrown ruins of urban wastelands. In some cities the urban foxes have been well established for several generations, and they may even outnumber fox populations found in surrounding country areas.

Gulls perform a valuable task as scavengers on many rubbish tips

Rubbish tips

Domestic refuse contains a considerable amount of discarded foodstuff, and for this reason rubbish tips are very attractive to gulls, starlings, members of the crow family and other birds. Some gulls, notably the herring gull, have greatly increased in numbers in recent years, and this may be because they can find abundant food on rubbish tips all the year round.

A quite remarkable variety of plants, both native and foreign, can be found growing on refuse tips. The more exotic plants arrive by way of packets of cage bird food and certain industries, like carpet manufacturers, which import raw wool that often has seeds entangled in it. Decaying rubbish generates heat, and this encourages the growth of plants from warmer parts of the world, although they are usually killed off by the first hard weather of winter.

One of the most common plants on rubbish tips is the tomato, which grows from seeds in rotten tomatoes thrown in dustbins or half-eaten sandwiches left in litter bins. Tomatoes are also common on sewage farms. These grow from seeds that have passed through the human gut. Many sewage farms still have settling beds into which sewage sludge is pumped, and the warm, damp conditions of such places support a wealth of invertebrate life which attracts birds such as gulls, lapwings and even some warblers.

The Great House and its Grounds

THERE are more than 1,500 country houses in Britain regarded as being of outstanding historical or architectural interest. It may no longer be true that the stately homes of England prove that the upper classes still have the upper hand, as Noel Coward wrote, but they remain among its glories.

Jacobean architecture is set off to perfection by the formal gardens at Blickling Hall in Norfolk

Gamekeepers

So far back in history does the role of the gamekeeper extend that Chaucer was writing of the well-known efficiency of the poacher turned gamekeeper in the 14th century. Poaching has always been both a crime and a sport in the countryside, and game laws severe and sometimes ferocious. As late as 1816 a law was passed which meant transportation for a cottager found with hare or rabbit nets upon him at night. Laws became increasingly humane later in the 19th century, but gamekeepers have always had something of a bad name for their hostility to trespassers who might disturb nesting pheasants, and because there are still those who consider birds of prey, badgers, otters and other creatures to be legitimate targets for poison or gun. Nevertheless, most gamekeepers have a profound, if paradoxical, love of the countryside and all wildlife. Certainly they understand it better than the majority of people who wander in their woods and across their carefully managed moors.

Whether newly affluent or of ancient lineage – and some of the finest houses were built by successful tradesmen and unscrupulous adventurers – the landowners of Britain have always shown a preference for living in the country rather than the town. Their houses were the centre of busy estates, the focus of local communities. Their estates provided parkland for their deer, warrens for their rabbits, coverts and woodland for their foxes and pheasants. The houses themselves reflected, and in most cases still reflect, the interests and affections of their owners. In France, where the landowning tradition is very different, historic châteaux are often lifeless shells.

From sturdy hall to glazed splendour

Even in Roman times the provincial villa and its estate was a key element in the countryside, and the great halls of the landed Saxon thegns were the basis for the Norman manors that supplanted them, such as the two-storeyed Norman house so remarkably preserved at Boothby Pagnell in Lincolnshire.

After the Reformation the squires and gentry of England began to build splendid homes for themselves and their descendants. One of many houses to show the transition and accumulation of styles from the early 14th century over several succeeding centuries is Ightham Mote in Kent, so called not because of its moat, but because it was once the venue for the fortnightly 'moot' or court of local justice held by the lord of the manor.

Deer hunting was the sport of kings and noblemen. They were hunted mainly in forests and chases; deer parks, of which there were more than 700 by 1580, were principally a way of keeping deer conveniently close and confined should venison be required. Severe laws governed all game. A statute of 1389 forbade any man with less than 40 shillings a year in land from

Parts of Ightham Mote date back to the 14th century

Dovecotes
Dovecotes were used by the Romans, but they were introduced to Britain by the Normans as a part of their manorial domestic economy like rabbit warrens and fish ponds. Doves breed prolifically: the dovecote in Dunster, Somerset, part of the medieval priory, is said to have provided 200 squabs (baby birds) a week. At Hinton Charterhouse near Bath, the library of the Carthusian monks who built Hinton Priory is next to the dovecote, so that it is possible to imagine how the cooing of the doves must have soothed that silent world of scholarship and illustration. Dovecotes were used until the end of the 18th century, and many remain, often sturdy examples of domestic architecture like those at Basing House in Hampshire and at Willington in Bedfordshire. Many were built into the gable ends of granaries and barns – often to the annoyance of the tenant farmer thus afflicted with a scourge for his corn.

Rhododendrons

Rhododendron ponticum grows wild in many parts of the country

One of the most ubiquitous plants to be found in the parks and gardens of Britain, and particularly around large country houses, is the rhododendron. There are about 200 varieties, many of which are marvellously displayed in such landscaped gardens as those of Stourhead and Longleat in Wiltshire. In late April, May and June these massive evergreen shrubs, often more than 20 feet high, are covered in heavy clustered flowers of every shade from mauve through scarlet, pink and rose to cream and apricot. Some were introduced from Asia, others from Europe as early as the 17th century; but it was a species from southern Spain, *Rhododendron ponticum*, which was found growing wild and has continued to do so with greatest vigour and success in the British Isles. It likes a sandy or peaty soil without lime, and when well suited it can become so dominant that other native plants cannot withstand its bulk and shade. In many woods its flowers are a familiar sight in late spring, and it is very difficult to control.

keeping sporting nets or dogs. But there was still a lot of wild moor and fen to poach and in any case poaching was not just the livelihood of a few but the sport of all classes, including infuriated farmers who preferred to see the lord of the manor's doves on his table rather than in his corn. Rabbits were common prey, and everyone, lord or peasant, snared and limed small birds such as larks and thrushes.

The Elizabethans liked to romanticize their medieval past and made elaborate additions to many existing houses. In Cheshire William Moreton turned Little Moreton Hall into a dazzling black and white tracery which must have appeared as magical as the designs of aces, spades and clubs on the new court playing cards just introduced. Imaginative design was linked to marvellous craftsmanship and new materials. The use of window glass reached such extravagant heights at Hardwick Hall, an astonishing example of Tudor symmetry which still glitters above the M1 in Derbyshire, that people said of it 'more glass than wall'.

Classical ideals and romantic dreams

Comfort and cool classicism marked the 17th century. In 1617 Inigo Jones introduced a completely new style when he began the pale and graceful Queen's House at Greenwich. At Chatsworth that serene spirit is allied to a later Baroque ebullience, ultimately fulfilled at Sir John Vanbrugh's Blenheim Palace, built for the first Duke of Marlborough. The setting of a house was becoming important. Levens Hall in Westmorland has one of the few surviving examples of 17th-century topiary, an almost sinisterly dark and massive company of abstract shapes of clipped yew and box, and at Chatsworth there is a sparkling stepped cascade and a great still canal to mirror its silvery stone.

The 18th and 19th centuries, the one marked by the wealth of the landowner, the other by the rising fortunes of the industrialist, saw great new houses built for fancy, fashion and ostentation. They varied from elegant concoctions like Robert Adam's Kedleston Hall to romantic fantasies like Horace Walpole's Gothic Strawberry Hill and the Duke of Rutland's Belvoir Castle, from the Palladian tranquillity of Stourhead and its garden in Wiltshire to the vigorous Victorian mansion of Cragside, built for Lord Armstrong in 1870.

The picturesque and the grandiose, as well as the Italianate and formal, influenced the grounds of great houses. Whole landscapes were recreated by men like Humphry Repton and Capability Brown, so called because of his habit of estimating the 'capabilities' of a stretch of countryside. Parks and gardens were planted with so confident a vision that their owners never saw them become reality, and we are lucky to see them at – and often past – maturity.

Parkland

THE illustration shows an area of mature parkland with a stately home in the background. Hundreds of such parks were created in the 18th and 19th centuries by landscape artists like Capability Brown. Such undertakings often involved remodelling the existing landscape; rivers and streams were dammed to make lakes, thousands of trees were planted, and sometimes whole villages were moved to new sites so as not to interrupt the newly-created vista from the great house. One of the trees frequently planted to terminate a vista was the lovely Cedar of Lebanon, thought to have been introduced into England by John Evelyn in the 17th century. Horse chestnuts, originally from Greece, were often planted in long avenues and look their best when covered in blossom in May.

Key

1 Jackdaw
2 Spotted flycatcher
3 Green woodpecker
4 Sweet chestnut
5 Fallow deer
6 Mistle thrush
7 Hardheads (*also known as lesser knapweed, June–September*)
8 Teazel (*July–September*)
9 Cotton thistle (*also known as Scotch thistle, July–September*)
10 Crow
11 Rook
12 Cedar of Lebanon
13 Swift (*summer visitor*)
14 Crested dog's tail
15 Pheasant (*cock*)
16 Jacob's sheep
17 Creeping bent grass
18 Starling
19 Chickweed (*February–November*)
20 Mute swan
21 Pheasant (*hen*)
22 Weeping willow
23 Stitchwort (*April–June*)
24 Tufted duck
25 Canada goose
26 Highland cow
27 Stock dove
28 Collared dove

The animals and plants are not drawn to scale. Plants are in flower during the months shown in brackets

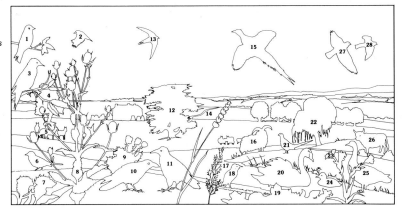

89

Churches

Northleach Church contains many brasses commemorating wool merchants who contributed to its rebuilding in the 15th century

Nonconformist chapels and meeting houses

Although there were sects which broke away from the established church as early as the mid 16th century, there are no Nonconformist places of worship in Britain dating from before 1650. The most distinctive early chapels are the meeting houses of the Quakers, whose doctrine forbade decoration and ostentation. Quaker Meeting Houses, like the one at Jordans near Beaconsfield, built in 1688, have a quiet beauty achieved with no embellishments.

Early Methodist chapels (the first one was built in 1739) were designed as preaching houses with as many seats as possible. They did not have altars or decoration since at that time Methodism was still part of the Church of England and the parish churches contained such things.

During the 19th century there was a tremendous upsurge in Nonconformity and hundreds of chapels were built. They are lasting tributes both to the craftsmen who built them and to the congregations which clubbed together to pay for them. They are usually worth investigating since many have interiors that are sober, but delightful, masterpieces.

WHETHER it stood boldly in the centre of the village, or nestled in woods near the manor house, the church was an integral part of every medieval village scene. It was not set aside purely for the celebration of Holy Communion and other religious activities, but was the focus of the village's social life, being the setting for meetings and gatherings of a purely secular kind. In less settled parts of the country the church was also a place of refuge in times of unrest and invasion; hence the fortress-like appearance of many churches in the West Country, Wales and the borderlands. The very first churches were built in wood, but most were rebuilt in stone between the Saxon period and the Norman Conquest.

Statements in stone

For hundreds of years the church was probably the only stone building for miles, except perhaps for the castle of the local baron. The villagers lived in hovels or bothies constructed from wood, thatch or turf, and even the hall of the lord of the manor, also a wooden building, would, to modern eyes, resemble a draughty and smoke-filled barn. All of the village's pride and love went into the church – its permanence and solidity reflecting the strength and glory of God, and contrasting with the fleeting nature of life in the harsh medieval world. Even comparatively poor villages endowed their churches with gold Communion vessels and finely worked vestments for the parish priest.

With the great wealth brought to England by wool and cloth during the 14th and 15th centuries came many of the lovely vernacular buildings which are thought of as being typically English, and hundreds of village churches were rebuilt or extended by rich merchants and guilds. They are great statements in stone, wood and glass that speak as much about the aspirations and power of their builders as they do about the everlasting love and divine spirit of God.

Around the churchyard
Round churchyards are not uncommon, and these may indicate that the church was built within a circular pagan temple. Prehistoric standing stones are incorporated into some churchyard walls, as is the case at Ysbyty Cynfyn, near Aberystwyth in mid Wales.

Carved with intricate geometrical patterns, this Celtic cross stands in the churchyard at Nevern in Dyfed

New churches in a new age

There was another tremendous burst of church-building in the 19th century. Throughout the 17th and 18th centuries churches were built in a variety of styles, often based on classical architecture, but there was no demand for large numbers of new churches. The increase in population, and national wealth, throughout the 19th century spurred Parliament, Church authorities and architects to build hundreds of new churches and to remodel many old ones.

Most of the new churches were built in the rapidly expanding cities and towns, but country landowners – both the established local gentry and the newly-rich industrial magnates – commissioned architects like Gilbert Scott, George Edmund Street and William Burges to rebuild local parish churches. Such architects were highly individualistic, rejecting the classical forms of architecture and freely re-working various Gothic motifs. The churches they built, rich in texture and design, re-stated in original ways medieval concepts of the mystery of worship and the grandeur of God's houses.

Michael churches

Britain's churches are as varied and distinctive as the landscapes in which they stand. Although most are closely connected with village or town, there are a good number which stand isolated, seemingly far from any community. Many of these have an extraordinary and compelling presence. Those on prominent hilltops are usually dedicated to St Michael, the archangel who was Captain of the Heavenly Host. In early Christian communities he was associated with Osiris, the Light of the Sun in Egyptian religion, and chapels dedicated to him were built in prominent places to catch the first rays of the morning sun. One of the most magical of Michael churches is that crowning the summit of Glastonbury Tor in Somerset.

Britain's churches contain one of the finest collections of art in the world. They have lent beauty and character to the landscape for over 1,000 years, and they are still the most important architectural components in the countryside scene.

Lychgates – roofed coverings over the churchyard entrance – date mostly from the Victorian period. They usually stand on the site of a church stile, where the priest met the funeral party and the corpse (lych means corpse), and where the burial service began.

The shafts of medieval preaching crosses can still be seen in some churchyards. Their heads, often depicting the Crucifixion, may have been broken off by Puritans during the 17th century. Memorial stones dating from the Dark Ages are occasionally found. Often these were incorporated into the fabric of the church at some stage and were rediscovered by Victorian restorers.

Few tombstones in the churchyard date from before the 17th or 18th century. Before that time the rich and powerful were buried inside the church, while the poor were buried in the yard in unmarked graves. The best tombstones are usually found near the south door, the main entrance to the church. Paupers, strangers and other unfortunates were buried on the north side, often near the churchyard wall. It is frequently the case that the north side of a church will have retained more early features, perhaps a Norman window or grotesque gargoyle, than the south side. This is because any available money was spent improving and 'modernizing' the south side, which was seen by one and all, while the north side, perhaps shaded by huge yew trees, was left largely unaltered.

Sports and Customs

Above: children dancing round a maypole is one of the most enchanting sights of spring. Like all May Day festivities it was once partly a fertility custom and partly a way of expressing the renewal of the earth after the cold and darkness of winter

Well Dressing

The springing of water from the ground has always been symbolic of life, and throughout the centuries people have expressed a fascination with wells. Springs and wells were identified with deities, to whom offerings were given, and whose healing powers were often said to reside in the water. In Derbyshire in midsummer the wells are dressed as a Christian custom today, and at Tissington they have been so decorated since at least the 18th century when the ceremony was revived out of an older custom that may date back to 1350 or before. The task involves making an initial design, perhaps of a cathedral, or a scene from the Bible, on a clay panel, and then after weeks of preparation local people all join to press each flower petal, seedhead or leaf into place. On the day of the blessing the picture is perfect, and the damp clay in which the flowers are pressed keeps them looking fresh for a considerable time.

FEW sights so vividly establish the English scene as a game of cricket on a village green, and since the first recognized cricket club was established at Hambledon in Hampshire in 1750 they have become part of country life. The local pub has always been part of the ritual, and in winter games such as darts, skittles and shove ha'penny, all going back over centuries, have replaced the summer cricket with their own fiercely competitive local leagues.

The sporting life

Sports have always been a part of rural life, many involving hunting, and often sharply divided between the legitimate pleasures of the gentry and the illicit nightly forays of the poacher. Angling is still the most popular participant sport in Britain, with competitions throughout the coarse-fishing season to see who can land the heaviest weight of chubb, roach or perch. More exclusive is fly-fishing on some of the most beautiful rivers anywhere. In the Welsh hills and Lake District fells many farmers own a solitary 'trencher-fed' hound with which to hunt the fox on foot. These hounds normally hunt with a pack of other trencher-fed hounds, which are kept and fed on farms rather than conventional communal hunt kennels. The hare, too, is pursued by foot-followers behind a pack of beagles – unlike the fox the hare tends to run in a circle. Foxhunting and staghunting on horseback, like shooting, is enthusiastically followed in most counties, and rough shooting with just a dog and gun to pot a few pigeons or a rabbit is one of the commonest pastimes of those who work and live in the country. In the Lake District, especially at the well-known Grasmere Sports (held in August) fell-running and hound-trailing are prime attractions, as is the local wrestling between burly contestants.

Customs through the year

Spring, as the season of renewal, is a time of ritual. May, which was deeply significant long before Christianity, is celebrated with processions, May Queen crownings and maypoles throughout the country, with a particularly fine ceremony at Knutsford in Cheshire. At Helston in Cornwall the famous Furry Dance takes place early in May, and although crowds come to watch the dances through the decorated streets it is still very much a local occasion. In Cornwall too is found the Hobby Horse of Padstow, a black

Left: Morris dancers at Thaxted in Essex. By tradition the dancers are men who wear decorated hats, flowers, ribbons and bells

Below: Padstow's hobby horse. Like many ancient customs this one is probably not clearly understood by either those who perform it or those who watch it, but it is nonetheless a compelling and often frightening event

canvas apparition with tail and grotesque mask which dances, dies and leaps to life again surrounded by its sinister attendants and musicians as it parades through the streets of the town. It survives today with another at Minehead in Somerset, compellingly mysterious but undoubtedly a fertility symbol. So too is the charming May Queen herself – the dances performed round village maypoles today were once much less demure.

Morris dancing, which often accompanies these ceremonies, is itself an ancient fertility rite. There are more than 200 teams of morris dancers in Britain and they can be seen throughout the year, especially at village fêtes in summer.

Summer has its own rituals, including the dressing of the wells in Derbyshire, and the Summer Solstice at Stonehenge when 20th-century Druids watch the sunrise on Midsummer's Day morning. The dying of the year brings darker rituals, like Hallowe'en or All Hallows' Eve on 31 October, with its candlelit masks made from hollowed-out turnips.

In Scotland, New Year takes precedence over Christmas, with First Footing being a major ceremony: a dark-haired man, preferably a stranger, brings luck if he is the first person to enter a house on New Year's Day. Fire is an element in many rituals in the north, with great bonfires in Wick, and at Allendale in Northumberland young men balance lighted tar barrels on their heads. At Lerwick, the capital of the Shetland Islands, people celebrate their Viking ancestors and the return of the sun at the true Yuletide, towards the end of January, with torchlit processions and a burning Viking galley.

The year sobers with Plough Sunday in January, when church services mark the new cycle of spring ploughing, sowing and harvest.

Up Helly Aa
The dramatic ceremony of Up Helly Aa takes place in Lerwick in the Shetland Isles on the last Tuesday in January, the ancient time of Scandinavian Yule celebrations. It once had barbaric elements, with sacrifices made, and even today it is a wild ritual, commemorating the final feast day in the house of the pagan gods, possibly the burning of the boats of the Viking settlers here. Men march with burning torches through the town, carrying a 30-foot-long model of a Viking galley which is eventually burned upon the shore to the sound of chanting 'up helly aa'.

Rural Crafts

THE Old English word 'craft' originally meant 'strength', and the true strength of any man or woman once lay in the skill of hand and eye. Craftsmen have always been members of an elite, so much so that in medieval times the craft guilds were powerful forces in the land. Mechanization and mass production have gradually diminished that power, but today there is a revival of respect not only for the individual craftsmen but also for the products of his skill.

Scythe-making

The village blacksmith once included scythes among the many tools he made and repaired. The scythe was always one of the most important tools in the countryside, used for cutting hay, reaping corn and manicuring the lawns of great houses. In the late 18th century scythe-making became identified with one area of the country and a particular family: the village of Belbroughton in North Worcestershire, and the Waldrons who made it a centre for the craft until the 1950s. Curiously enough the word scythe was specifically applied to the blade: the curved wooden handles or 'sneads' were locally made or imported wholesale from Scotland, and at one time from as far afield as the North American colonies. The 19th-century factory-made scythe blades were considered inferior to those made by the local blacksmith, as they consisted mostly of steel plate reinforced by an iron strip. The use of the scythe required a great deal of skill and good scythemen were very much in demand at harvest time.

Thatching

The thatcher was once a key figure in the rural community. Not only did houses and barns have to be well roofed against the British weather, but so did straw stacks and hayricks after harvest. Thatching is essentially a skill acquired through practical experience, and distinctive styles have been handed down in various parts of the country. There is scope for personal artistry in the finishing of roof ridges, eaves and gables, and many thatchers add their own trademark by way of a cross or a pair of pheasants on the roof.

Wheat straw is still the most widely used material for thatching, although reeds, which demand a slightly different technique, last longer – about 60 years for a good reed roof. Best of all are Norfolk reeds, although current supply hardly keeps up with demand.

The loose straw is moistened with water, straightened into yealms (Old English for handful) and neatly bound with either twine or a straw bond. The thick yealms are laid close and overlapping and fixed with pegs, or spars, made of hazel or willow. Most thatched roofs are decoratively finished with hazel rods which pattern the ridges and eaves as they secure the yealms of straw. Estimating just how many yealms of straw and bundles of spars might be needed for a roof is an important part of the thatcher's ability, especially today when most straw is baled after harvest instead of being stooked in the fields. The long straw, unbaled, is needed for thatching, and has to be specially cut for the purpose. Nevertheless, there are some 750 thatchers kept busy in Britain today.

Wagons and wheelwrights

Transport by water was easier than on land in Celtic times, although two-wheeled carts drawn by oxen were well established by the Anglo-Saxons. Farm carts and four-wheeled wagons gradually developed to the point where different areas of the country, and indeed local districts, had their own styles of horse-drawn vehicle. It was possible to identify a Cotswold or Herefordshire wagon at a glance. Drawn by teams of horses, they were the pride of the craftsmen wagonmakers and could last 100 years; many in use today were thus built in the 19th century.

Wagons were objects of enormous pride, but wheels were the bread and butter of craftsmen, since the body of the wagon would outlast several sets of wheels. The wood used by the wheelwright was important. The nave, or boss of the wheel, strengthened with iron, was always made of elm, because only elm could stand up to the mortising of the spokes that fanned out from it. The spokes themselves were of oak, and the curved outer wheel, tyred in iron clamped redhot to its surface, was made of segments of ash, elm or beech.

Baskets and boats

Allied to thatching is basket-making, one of the oldest crafts in the world. It dates back to at least 5,000 BC. Because it depended so much on nimble fingers and so little on any other equipment, just good canes or reeds, it has always had a place in providing anything from beds to boxes, roofs to animal cages. Baskets are simply very good receptacles for storage and carrying things, and the willow osiers used for them grow quickly and easily. On the lowland levels of Somerset basket-making flourishes, using local willows.

In Sussex, a particular type of basket has become identified with the county. The spacious trug was much admired by Queen Victoria when it was displayed at the Great Exhibition in 1851. Ideal for carrying anything which requires some care in handling, it is made from flat straps of wood, steamed to make them flexible, and attached to the wide rim with nails.

The word 'trug' is based on the Old English name for a woven boat, a coracle. Such boats date back to Celtic times and probably earlier. In recent years a practical demonstration has proved that the Celtic Irish Saint Brendan could have sailed across the Atlantic in such a craft. Made very much like baskets, usually of ash or hazel and willow wickerwork, traditionally covered in animal hides (though many are now covered in man-made materials), coracles can still be seen in use on the Teifi and Tywi rivers of Wales, where a few fishermen retain licences to net salmon. Occasionally coracles of a distinctive type can be seen on the upper Severn in Shropshire.

Above: a Somerset basket weaver

Left: a Victorian barge wagon

Rural Crafts

Above: an Oxfordshire saddlemaker surrounded by the tools of his trade

Right: anvils are perhaps the most important tools of both the farrier and the blacksmith

Working with leather

The horse was of course an essential element in transport, replacing the ox in medieval times. Saddlery and harness-making, like the crafts of the cart- and carriage-builder and the wheelwright, were much respected in the past and are continuing steadily today. Working with leather to make an intricate harness which must not only be durable and efficiently engineered but comfortable, is a painstaking – and sometimes painful – task. From the harness of heavy draught horses with their massive and carefully tailored collars to the lighter but no less complex driving harness, a vast and awesome range of implements is required. They vary from awls, punches and huge clamps to special compasses, mallets made of lignum vitae and eight-inch curved needles.

Blacksmith and farrier

THE titles blacksmith and farrier both derive from words once used for ironworking, smith being Old English in origin and farrier Norman French. Today there is a clear distinction between the two: the blacksmith works in iron and other metals, and the farrier, often with a mobile forge, deals specifically with the shoeing of the horse.

The blacksmith's forge, while always being available for shoeing horses, particularly local draught animals, was nevertheless at least as important for metalworking. Iron was the smith's stock in trade, heated in his hooded furnace and set sizzling to cool in a quenching tank, beaten upon an anvil which rested on a block of oak or elm to give it 'life' and make it more responsive to the blacksmith's touch. The anvil seen today was perfected in England in the Middle Ages. It can weigh more than two hundredweight and produce as true a ringing note as a bell when struck. A traditional blacksmith's shop was littered with tools which could be used for any conceivable job. Many blacksmiths made their own tools, and often showed the pride which they took in producing them by making them more attractive than practical use demanded and by stamping their initials on them. Today's blacksmiths continue the work of their predecessors in producing fine decorative and ornamental ironwork; and some repair tractors and other farm machinery in the same way that the smiths of yesterday mended wagons, carts, and ploughs.

A Country Pathfinder

Gazetteer of places to visit, directory of
the protected countryside, useful addresses and
hints on what to do and what to take
to make the countryside more enjoyable.

Gazetteer

The gazetteer which follows is a selection of some of the most interesting museums, stately homes and countryside areas in Britain. There are, of course, many hundreds of others, and details of these can be obtained from publications like the AA's guide to Stately Homes, Museums, Castles and Gardens in Britain, and from the organizations whose names and addresses are given on pages 120–121.

Opening times of such places as stately homes and museums should always be checked before visiting to avoid disappointment. Many nature reserves have public footpaths or waymarked trails leading through them, and these should always be kept to, since the essence of such reserves is that areas of them should remain undisturbed. Irreparable damage can be done to reserves by those who, perhaps quite innocently, wander over them at will. Access to some reserves, or parts of reserves, is often limited, and these details should always be checked before making a visit.

Wherever you are in the countryside always follow the Country Code (given on page 119) and remember that the countryside can be damaged just as easily by misplaced good intentions as by deliberate vandalism.

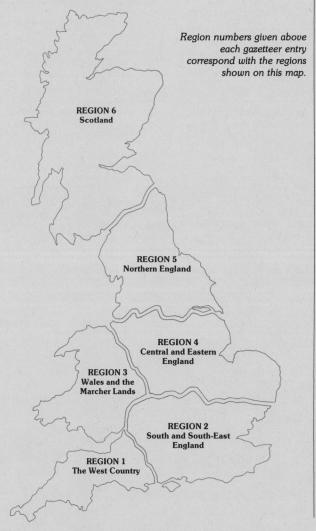

Region numbers given above each gazetteer entry correspond with the regions shown on this map.

REGION 6
Scotland

REGION 5
Northern England

REGION 4
Central and Eastern
England

REGION 3
Wales and the
Marcher Lands

REGION 2
South and South-East
England

REGION 1
The West Country

AGRICULTURAL MUSEUMS

REGION 3
Acton Scott, Salop
Acton Scott Working Farm Museum
The farm lies 3 miles south of Church Stretton. Agricultural practice, as it was at the turn of the century, is demonstrated here. Rare breeds of farm animals are stocked and all work is done by hand or horse. Visitors are invited to participate in some of the farm work and craft demonstrations take place at weekends.

REGION 6
Auchindrain, Strath
Argyll Museum of Farming Life
Situated 6 miles south of Inveraray on the A83. The museum is actually a deserted farming village in which the crofts have been restored. Farm tools and domestic equipment of the period are on display.

REGION 6
Auchindrain, Strath
Open-Air Museum
A folk life museum on an ancient communal tenancy farm. The original 18th- and 19th-century buildings are being restored and furnished. Traditional crops and livestock can be seen, and there is also a display centre.

REGION 5
Coulby Newham, Cleveland
Newham Grange Farm Agricultural Museum
Farming in Cleveland through the ages is the theme of this museum, which is part of a working farm stocked with rare breeds of sheep, cattle, pigs and poultry.

REGION 4
Easton, Suffolk
Easton Farm Park
The farm park includes some rare breeds of farm animals and a Victorian dairy where visitors can watch milking take place each afternoon. Among the other attractions are the country bygones and the bee-keeping exhibition.

REGION 2
Guiting Power, Glos
Cotswold Farm Park
Begun in 1970 as a centre for the Rare Breeds Survival Trust, all animals in the park are specimens of ancient breeds of farm livestock. Many of the animals are used for cross-breeding to improve modern farmstock. There is an exhibition about the development of British livestock breeding on a typical Cotswold Farm. This is one of the most fascinating and important collections in the country.

REGION 6
Harray, Orkney
Corrigall Farm Museum
This restored Orkney farmstead dates from the mid 19th century. Exhibits include a grain-drying kiln, domestic furnishings and implements of the period.

Huntly, Grampian
Agriculture Museum
Agricultural exhibits including farm implements, horse and cattle equipment, butter and cheese-making utensils, corn dollies and many hand-tools are on show in this fascinating museum.

REGION 3
Kidderminster, Herefs & Worcs
Country Centre
Over 60 horse-powered farming implements gathered from all over Britain, are on display in this private collection, as well as examples of saddler's, blacksmith's and wheelwright's shops and general farming tools.

REGION 4
Laxton, Notts
Laxton Village
The village lies between Newark-on-Trent and Retford, 4 miles east of Ollerton. Although not a museum, Laxton is one of the most important and fascinating agricultural sites in the country, for here the land is still farmed on the medieval 'open field' system. There are three huge fields, each of which is divided into strips that are cultivated individually.

REGION 5
Newton, Northumb
Hunday National Tractor and Farm Museum
Original 19th-century stone buildings house a collection of over 250 tractors and engines which trace the development of agriculture from 1900 to the post-war period. Also on show are small hand tools, harness, farm and dairy equipment, and an 1835 Bingfield steam engine and thresher. Joiner's and blacksmith's shops, a farmhouse kitchen and many domestic items are on show in the display area. Farm animals are also kept.

REGION 4
Oakham, Leics
Rutland Farm Park
This is part of Catmose Farm, a working farm with rare and commercial breeds of farm livestock as well as Shetland and Exmoor ponies. It is set in 18 acres of park and woodland which includes a stream, walks and picnic sites.

REGION 3
Plwmp, Dyfed
West Wales Farm Park
Belted Welsh and White Park cattle and Manx Loghtan sheep are just some of the rare breeds of farm livestock that can be seen here. There are also modern breeds of farm animals and fowl.

REGION 2
Sedlescombe, E Sussex
Nortons Farm Museum and Farm Trail
Located 4½ miles north-west of Hastings on the A21. This museum depicts the 'cart horse era', with fine displays of carts, ploughs and hand tools. The Farm Trail takes visitors around the fruit and arable farm, where cart horses are still used.

REGION 1
Shebbear, Devon
Alscott Farm Agricultural Museum
This museum houses a remarkable collection of vintage farm tractors, ploughs, dairy and household implements, photographs and information on north Devon's agricultural past. There is a Wallis and Stevens traction engine on show, and a special exhibition including a unique scale model of an Edwardian travelling fair with contemporary photographs and original circus posters.

REGION 2
Shovewell, Isle of Wight
Yafford Water Mill Farm Park
Set in attractive surroundings, with a large mill pond and stream, this 19th-century mill contains much of the original machinery. There is also a collection of farm implements, wagons and tractors.

REGION 4
Skegness, Lincs
Church Farm Museum
The lifestyle of the 19th-century Lincolnshire farmer is recreated in a restored farmhouse and outbuildings. Exhibits include farm implements and machinery, and domestic and household equipment. Craftsmen can be seen at work on Sundays during the summer.

REGION 1
Staverton, Devon
Riverford Farm
The highlight of a visit to this farm is a tour of the farm on a tractor-drawn trailer. During the tour visitors can see the day-to-day work in progress, the farm animals, and watch a weaver and wood-turner at work. There is also an exhibition of the history of rural life and farming.

REGION 1
Summercourt, Cornwall
Dairyland & Cornish Country Life Museum
A large herd of cows is milked each day at Dairyland in one of Europe's most up-to-date rotary milking parlours. The museum includes some fascinating working exhibits. Game birds and wildfowl are on view. Milkings 3.15–4.30pm.

REGION 2
Tilford, Surrey
Old Kiln Agricultural Museum
A fine collection of farm implements and machinery can be seen here along with examples of the crafts and trades allied to farming. Larger exhibits are displayed in pleasant garden and woodland surroundings, covering some 10 acres. Old farm buildings house the smithy, a wheelwright's shop and a collection of hand tools.

REGION 1
Wembworthy, Devon
Ashley Countryside Collection
Nearly 50 different breeds of British sheep can be seen here, including all the rare breeds. Exhibits include wheelwrights', coopers', blacksmiths' and other country craftsmen's tools and workshops, and there is a fleece exhibition.

REGION 2
Witney, Oxfordshire
Cogges Manor Farm
Set in the Edwardian period, the farm exhibits the agriculture of Oxfordshire together with local breeds of livestock. Farmhouse kitchens, a dairy and walled gardens can also be seen. Agricultural and craft demonstrations take place at weekends.

INDUSTRIAL MUSEUMS

REGION 4
Alvingham, Lincs
Alvingham Water Mill
This 18th-century water-powered cornmill has been restored as a working museum. A mill has stood on this site since Domesday and it was once used by the monks of Alvingham Abbey. The present machinery, which dates from about 1782, is powered by one of the few remaining breast wheels.

REGION 2
Amberley, W Sussex
Amberley Chalk Pits Museum
Situated in a 36-acre former chalk quarry and limeworks off the B2139, this museum has been established to portray the industrial past of south-east England. Exhibits include the original limekilns and there is also a cobbler's shop, machine shop and brick-making display. Nature and geology trail.

REGION 4
Barlaston, Staffs
Wedgwood Museum and Visitor Centre
Traditional skills in the production of the famous Wedgwood pottery can be seen in the craft demonstration area, while the museum displays a comprehensive collection of the works of the Wedgwood factory from 1750. Wedgwood's history is also portrayed on film.

REGION 5
Beamish, Co Durham
North of England Open-Air Museum
Northern people and their way of life is the subject of this, England's first open-air museum. Buildings of all kinds have been rebuilt and furnished on a 200-acre site. A major feature of the museum is the colliery, complete with a row of miner's cottages, where visitors can take a trip underground and see the coal. Steam locomotives and trams take visitors across the site to Home Farm where farm tools and machinery, carts and farm animals can be seen. There is also a North Eastern Railway station and a collection of different forms of transport. Demonstrations of traditional crafts take place.

REGION 2
Buckler's Hard, Hants
Maritime Museum
This museum is located in the village where wooden warships, including vessels for Nelson's fleet, were once built from New Forest oak.

REGION 3
Dre-Fach Felindre, Dyfed
Museum of the Woollen Industry
This museum is a branch of the National Museum of Wales, administered by the Welsh Folk Museum. It occupies part of the Cambrian Mills, a working mill, and its collection of textile machinery dates from the 18th century. The exhibition traces the development of the industry from the Middle Ages to the present day.

REGION 3
Ironbridge, Salop
Ironbridge Gorge Museum
Within an area of some 6 square miles in the Severn Gorge stands a unique series of monuments to the Industrial Revolution. The first iron bridge in the world is here, surrounded by a number of industrial museums:

Blists Hill Open Air Museum
The local industries of iron, coal and clay are recreated here on a 42-acre woodland site. Exhibits also illustrate the living and working conditions of the 18th-century inhabitants of the area.

Coalbrookdale Museum and Furnace Site
The blast furnace where Abraham Darby perfected the technique of smelting iron ore using coke as a fuel can be seen here. Associated with the furnace is a museum of iron and steel which includes a feature on the Coalbrookdale Company whose work includes the iron gates which stand between Kensington Gardens and Hyde Park in London, and the Ironbridge itself.

Coalport China Works Museum
The world-famous china was produced here from the late 18th century to 1926. The original buildings now house workshops, social history displays and an exhibition of fine porcelain.

Severn Warehouse
This restored 19th-century building and its adjoining wharf is a Visitor Centre which introduces Ironbridge Gorge with slide shows, exhibits and displays.

REGION 3
Llangollen, Clwyd
Canal Exhibition Centre
Visitors to the Centre on The Wharf may enjoy a trip on a horse-drawn passenger boat through the beautiful Vale of Llangollen. The museum illustrates the fascinating story of Britain's canal era by means of static and working models, photographs, murals, films and slides.

REGION 4
Nottingham, Notts
Canal Museum
The ground floor and wharfage of this late 19th-century warehouse is now the setting for a museum devoted to the history of the River Trent from the Ice Age to the present day. Displays include information on local canal and river navigation, boats, bridges, archaeology etc.

REGION 4
Nottingham, Notts
Industrial Museum
Nottingham's foremost industries, hosiery and lacemaking, are a major feature of this fascinating museum which is housed in an 18th-century stable block in Wollaton Park. Exhibits from the city's other industries include pharmaceutical, engineering, tobacco and printing equipment. New extensions house heavy agricultural machinery and a mid 19th-century beam pumping engine which can sometimes be seen in steam. Victorian street furniture is on display in the yard outside, along with a horse gin from a local coal mine.

REGION 6
Pitlochry, Tayside
Pitlochry Power Station Dam and Fish Pass
Access to the Power Station itself is not permitted but there is a permanent exhibition of hydro-electricity with an audio-visual presentation and a viewing gallery. Visitors may watch salmon swim up-river from the Fish Pass observation chamber – open during daylight hours.

REGION 1
St Austell, Cornwall
Wheal Martyn Museum
The story of Cornwall's china clay industry is told here on a fascinating open-air site. A complete clay works of the last century has been restored and huge granite-walled settling tanks, working water wheels and a wooden slurry pump can be seen. There are also indoor displays, a short slide and sound programme, and a working pottery to watch on display.

LOCAL HISTORY MUSEUMS

REGION 2
Alton, Hants
Curtis Museum
Displays of craft tools, dolls, toys and games as well as local geological, botanical, zoological and archaeological specimens and historical finds can be seen here.

REGION 2
Aylesbury, Bucks
Bucks County Museum
Two 15th-century houses and a former 18th-century grammar school house this museum. Displays relate to the geology, natural history, archaeology and history of the county. There are also costume exhibits and a Rural Life Gallery.

REGION 3
Caldicot, Gwent
Caldicot Castle
One of the many interesting features of this restored Norman castle is its local history museum. Exhibits include displays of rural crafts and costume.

REGION 2
Chelmsford, Essex
Chelmsford and Essex Museum
The museum, situated in Oaklands Park, includes exhibits relating to prehistoric and Roman Britain, as well as displays of costumes, coins, British birds and mammals, geology, ceramics and the work of local industries.

REGION 2
Chingford, Greater London
Queen Elizabeth's Hunting Lodge and Museum
The museum, in Epping Forest, is housed in a picturesque Tudor building dating from about 1543. Its exhibits relate the life of the animals, birds and plants that occupy Epping Forest, and man's association with them.

REGION 5
Clitheroe, Lancs
Clitheroe Castle Museum
Many items of local interest are housed in this museum attached to one of the oldest castles in Lancashire. The castle grounds command outstanding views of the Ribble valley.

REGION 2
Colchester, Essex
Natural History Museum
This museum is housed in what was once All Saints Church, a 15th-century structure with a fine flint tower. Displays feature the natural history of Essex with special reference to the Colchester area.

REGION 1
Dorchester, Dorset
Dorset County Museum
This museum houses a fine collection of prehistoric and Roman antiquities, and examples of the geology, natural history and rural crafts of the area. Thomas Hardy's manuscripts for *The Mayor of Casterbridge* are among the exhibits, as are relics of another Dorset man, the 19th-century poet William Barnes. Concerts, lectures and film shows are given here.

REGION 1
Helston, Cornwall
Helston Folk Museum
This folk museum, housed in the old Butter Market, covers local history and includes exhibits from the Lizard district.

101

REGION 4
Oakham, Leics
Rutland County Museum
This museum specializes in collections of local archaeology (particularly Roman and Anglo-Saxon), craft tools and local history. There is a Victorian shop, and its collections of agricultural implements and farm wagons are second in importance only to the collections held by the Museum of English Rural Life at Reading.

REGION 2
Sandown, Isle of Wight
Museum of Isle of Wight Geology
This interesting museum is housed in the local library and includes a fascinating collection of fossils and exhibits on the geology of the island.

REGION 2
Tilbury, Essex
Thurrock Riverside Museum
The history of the River Thames and the people of its riverside are the subjects of the museum which includes exhibits of ship and barge models and collections of old photographs.

REGION 4
Wisbech, Cambs
Wisbech and Fenland Museum
As well as general exhibits on the life of the Fens, this museum contains a fine collection of coins, ceramics, *objets d'art*, glass and pottery from Celtic, Roman and Saxon England.

REGION 2
Woodstock, Oxon
Oxfordshire County Museum
Located in a 16th- to 18th-century house, the museum tells the story of Oxfordshire from earliest times to the present day. The subjects covered include archaeology, industry, crafts and domestic life.

NATIONAL MUSEUMS

REGION 2
South Kensington, London SW7
Geological Museum
Britain Before Man and *British Fossils* are two recently-opened permanent exhibitions that tell the story of Britain's geological heritage and explain the country's regional geology.

As well as a famous collection of fine gem-stones, shown in their natural crystal form in the parent rock and in their final cut state, this fascinating museum includes a wealth of information on world geology.

REGION 2
South Kensington, London SW7
Natural History Museum
British birds, insects and wildlife, from prehistoric times to the present day, are displayed here against backgrounds that recreate their natural habitats. On the second floor, the Botanical Gallery includes outstanding dioramas illustrating various types of landscape and habitat.

REGION 2
Tring, Herts
The Zoological Museum
A branch of the British Natural History Museum, this museum specializes in mounted specimens of mammals, birds, insects and shells.

RURAL LIFE MUSEUMS

REGION 4
Alford, Lincs
Alford Manor House
The museum in this 16th-century manor house includes period shops, a school room, a maid's bedroom, a dairy, and agricultural and transport galleries.

REGION 4
Alford, Lincs
Mawthorpe Collection of Bygones
The collection comprises domestic and agricultural bygones including household equipment, shop displays and rural crafts. Special exhibits include vintage tractors, a large fairground organ and steam engines which are in steam on open days.

REGION 6
Anstruther, Fife
Scottish Fisheries Museum
This fascinating museum is housed in a group of 14th- to 18th-century buildings around a cobbled courtyard. Exhibits include fishing boats and gear, an early 20th-century fisherman's house and a marine aquarium.

REGION 2
Ashwell, Herts
Ashwell Village Museum
This early-Tudor timber-framed house, once the tithe office of the abbots of Westminster, is now a scheduled Ancient Monument. Exhibits include a display on village life from the Stone Age to the present day.

REGION 1
Bickleigh, Devon
Bickleigh Mill Craft Centre
One of the largest and most comprehensive working craft centres in the West Country, Bickleigh is powered by a picturesque old watermill which has been adapted to the production of craft work. Crafts include potting, glass-blowing, engraving, wood-turning, jewellery and corn dolly making. A farm, on which rare breeds of animals are kept, a fish farm and a museum are also part of the centre.

REGION 2
Breamore, Hants
Breamore House Countryside and Carriage Museums
Set in the grounds of a fine Elizabethan manor house, the Countryside Museum has exhibits arranged to illustrate the progress of farming through the seasons. There are interior displays of a farmworker's cottage before the advent of electricity, a forge, a wheelwright's shop, a dairy and a brewery. There is also a fine collection of farm machinery, including a splendid array of old tractors. A collection of livestock, including longhorn cattle and St Kilda, Soay and Jacob sheep can also be seen. The Carriage Museum boasts a fine collection of old coaches.

REGION 3
Bromsgrove, Herefs & Worcs
Avoncraft Museum of Buildings
Farm buildings, from the Middle Ages to the Industrial Revolution, have been saved from demolition and re-erected here. These include a thatched barn and a granary. Other buildings on show are timber-framed houses, nail and chainmaker's workshops, a cockpit theatre and a windmill, which can be seen working on certain days.

REGION 1

Buckfast, Devon
The Museum of Shellcraft
The museum, which is situated off the A38, boasts a large collection of shells from all over the world. Exhibits portray the shellcraft worker's art.

REGION 1

Calbourne, Isle of Wight
Calbourne Watermill and Rural Museum
A 17th-century watermill which is still in working order.

REGION 4

Cambridge, Cambs
Cambridge and County Folk Museum
Formerly the White Horse Inn, this museum features domestic objects, toys, furniture and agricultural tools, and a large collection of pictures and photographs relating to the county.

REGION 1

Camelford, Cornwall
North Cornwall Museum and Gallery
This museum of rural life depicts the life and work of the north Cornish people at the end of the 19th century. Exhibits include wheelwright's tools, a blacksmith's forge, cobbling implements, a dairy and domestic items.

REGION 3

Cenarth, Dyfed
Fishing Museum and Salmon Leap
Coracle making, fly-tying and poaching tackle are among the exhibits to be found in this rod and line museum. Other features of interest are an art gallery and the salmon leap.

REGION 6

Ceres, Fife
Fife Folk Museum
This is a regional, rural folk collection displayed in the historic Weigh House Cottages and terraced garden near Ceres Green.

REGION 1

Clevedon, Avon
Clevedon Craft Centre and Country Museum
To reach the Centre, turn off the B3130 opposite Clevedon Court and cross the M5. There are 12 studios with craftsmen available for discussion and commissioned work is undertaken. The museum specializes in country artefacts.

REGION 6

Colbost, Isle of Skye, Highland
The Skye Black House Folk Museum
On the B884. This museum is housed in a typical 19th-century house of the area, containing implements and furniture of bygone days with a peat fire burning throughout the day. A replica of an illicit whisky still stands behind the museum.

REGION 5

Cregneash, Isle of Man
Manx Open-air Folk Museum
This open-air museum comprises a group of traditional Manx cottages (some thatched), including a croft, a fisherman's home, a farmstead, a loom shed complete with hand-made loom, a lathe shed with treadle lathe, and a smithy.

REGION 6

Dervaig, Isle of Mull, Strath
Old Byre Visitor Centre
Situated 1 mile south off the B8073. This imaginative museum provides a reconstruction of the crofters' lives at the time of the clearances. Authentic cottage interiors include life-sized figures and animals. Audio-visual presentations take place every half hour.

REGION 6

Dunbeath, Highland
Laidhay Croft Museum
This 18th- to early 19th-century longhouse is a typical Caithness croft, with dwelling, byre and stable all under one thatched roof. It is furnished in traditional croft style.

REGION 2

Filkins, Oxon
Swinford Museum
The Swinford Museum displays old domestic articles, along with agricultural and rural craft tools. The village lock-up will be opened on request.

REGION 6

Gairloch, Highland
Gairloch Heritage Museum
The lifestyle of a typical West Highland village is portrayed in a converted farmstead at Achtercairn that now houses the museum. Exhibits date from earliest times to the 20th century and include a reconstruction of a crofter's room.

REGION 6

Glamis, Tayside
Angus Folk Museum
This folk collection is housed in a row of restored 19th-century cottages known as Kirkwynd Cottages. Exhibits include cottage furniture and domestic and agricultural equipment.

REGION 1

Glastonbury, Somerset
Somerset Rural Life Museum
Housed in the Abbey Barn, the museum contains relics of farming in Somerset and includes a display on the life of a farm labourer. There are exhibits on cider making, peat cutting and withy cutting and a typical farmhouse kitchen can be seen.

REGION 4

Gressenhall, Norfolk
Norfolk Rural Life Museum
This museum housed in an 18th-century workhouse, illustrates the county's history over the past 200 years. Particular emphasis is placed on agriculture, and displays of farming implements clearly explain their uses. Machinery and vehicles can be seen in the inner courtyards.

REGION 5

Halifax, W Yorks
West Yorkshire Folk Museum
Housed in the barn of 15th-century half-timbered Shibden Hall, this museum contains craft workshops and a collection of agricultural tools and machinery.

REGION 3

Hartlebury, Herefs & Worcs
Hereford and Worcester County Museum
Topics include country crafts and industries, period furnishings, costumes, toys and dolls. Horse-drawn vehicles such as gipsy caravans are kept here and there is also a forge and a wheelwright's shop to visit.

REGION 5

Hawes, N Yorks
Upper Dales Folk Museum
Exhibits relating to life in the Upper Dales can be seen in this small museum based on the collections of two Yorkshire women who spent many years researching the area. Unusual and interesting items related to rural skills include the equipment for making Wensleydale cheese.

REGION 5

Hutton-le-Hole, N Yorks
Ryedale Folk Museum
The antiquities of Ryedale, from prehistoric times to the beginning of this century, can be seen here. Exhibits include reconstructed cruck houses, a barn, a wheelshed and an Elizabethan furnace.

REGION 5

Kendal, Cumbria
Abbot Hall Museum of Lakeland Life and Industry
Housed in an 18th-century stable block, this museum covers all aspects of Lakeland life and trade, its social and economic history, with a special emphasis on fell farming. Exhibits include a dipping trough, early clipping stools, carts and sledges.

Kilmuir, Isle of Skye, Highland
Skye Cottage Museum
An unusual museum, consisting of four thatched cottages which portray the croft houses of a century ago. Exhibits include an interesting collection of old letters, papers and pictures. A selection of implements, tools and domestic items used by Highland men and women is also on show.

REGION 6
Kingussie, Highland
Highland Folk Museum
An interesting display of Highland crafts and furnishings are contained in this museum. Other attractions include a farming museum, a reconstructed Hebridean mill, and a primitive 'black house', set in 6 acres of garden.

REGION 3
Leominster, Herefs & Worcs
Leominster and District Folk Museum
The museum contains a fine display of smocks, coins, farm implements, corn dollies, tools and maps. All items of local historical interest have either been given to the museum, or lent, by local people.

REGION 4
Lincoln, Lincs
Museum of Lincolnshire Life
This museum has been designed to depict all aspects of life in the county from Elizabethan times to the present day. Exhibits include horse-drawn and passenger vehicles, industrial machinery and farm implements.

REGION 3
Llanvapley, Gwent
Gwent Rural Life Museum
This museum houses displays of domestic and rural bygones including craft tools and agricultural implements.

REGION 4
Martham, Norfolk
Countryside Collection
Part of the collection is a Museum of

Village Life which features historic agricultural equipment, vintage tractors, harnesses, wagons, old village trades and an original working forge. Most weekends during the season there are special attractions such as craft demonstrations and gymkhanas. There is also a vintage car rally and a steam rally. In the grounds are water gardens and a pheasant aviary.

REGION 5
Pickering, N Yorks
Beck Isle Museum of Rural Life
Once the home of leading agriculturalist William Marshall, this attractive Georgian house is now a folk museum relating to Pickering and the surrounding area. Exhibits are arranged thematically and include farming equipment, cooper's tools and a series of reconstructed shops.

REGION 3
St Fagan's, S Glam
Welsh Folk Museum
Situated 3 miles from the centre of Cardiff, this marvellous museum is an open-air branch of the National Museum of Wales. Exhibits include the 16th-century St Fagan's Castle, a woollen mill, a tannery, several old Welsh farmhouses and a chapel from the Vale of Teifi.

REGION 2
Singleton, W Sussex
Weald and Downland Open Air Museum
Historic buildings from Kent, Sussex, Surrey and Hampshire have been erected here alongside displays of traditional crafts and rural industries. Exhibits span the 14th to 19th centuries and include Tichfield market hall, a working watermill and the Hambrook barn, which houses an exhibition of building techniques and materials used since medieval times. All the buildings have been re-erected in a rural setting, and there is also a woodland trail which illustrates the crafts of coppicing and charcoal burning.

REGION 4
Stafford, Staffs
Staffordshire County Museum
The kitchen wing and stable block of impressive 17th-century Shugborough Hall at Great Haywood now house this county museum in which exhibits illustrate Staffordshire's agricultural development, social history and rural crafts. There is a fine collection of horse-drawn vehicles on display as well as an 18th-century brewhouse and laundry. Tamworth pigs, Longhorn cattle and Shropshire sheep are bred and shown here.

REGION 4
Stowmarket, Suffolk
Museum of East Anglian Life
Many threatened buildings of historic and architectural interest have been re-erected within the grounds of this open-air museum. As well as buildings such as a 14th-century farmhouse and a blacksmith's forge, the visitor can see collections of horse-drawn vehicles and farm implements.

REGION 2
Reading, Berks
Museum of English Rural Life
Established as a public museum in 1955, Reading University's Museum of English Rural Life in Whiteknights Park contains agricultural exhibits from all over England, dating from the late 19th and early 20th centuries. It is one of the most important museums of its kind in the world, and its reserve collections of photographs, catalogues and other material are unsurpassed. The exhibits which the public sees are beautifully arranged and displayed and cover every aspect of rural life, including country crafts, poaching and agricultural machinery.

REGION 2
Runwick, Surrey
Ridgeway House Farm Craft Centre
Ridgeway House is situated at the top of Runwick Lane, to the west of Farnham. Different country crafts are demonstrated each month and these include spinning, basket-making, patchwork and lace-making.

REGION 3
Wolvesnewton, Gwent
Model Farm Collection and Craft Centre
Situated 1½ miles off the B4235 at Llangwm, an 18th-century cruciform barn houses this fine collection of unusual and entertaining items used in everyday life from Queen Victoria's reign onwards. Also on show are agricultural implements, a Victorian bedroom and a medical section. Shop, craft workshops and gallery. Additional attractions include entertainment evenings, one-day craft courses and exhibitions.

REGION 5
Worsbrough, S Yorks
Worsbrough Mill Museum
Situated 2½ miles south of Barnsley, this museum consists of two mills, a 17th-century watermill and a 19th-century mill powered by a rare 1911 hot-bulb oil engine. Both mills stand within Worsbrough Country park. There are frequent special exhibitions and displays related to milling, agriculture and local history.

PARKS, GARDENS AND STATELY HOMES

REGION 1
Abbotsbury, Dorset
Abbotsbury Gardens
This magnificent stone-walled garden stands in 16 acres of grounds. Peacocks wander among fine trees and flowering shrubs.

REGION 6
Aberdeen, Grampian
Cruikshank Botanic Gardens
First developed at the end of the 19th century, the 7 acres of mature gardens belonging to the University of Aberdeen include rock and water gardens, a heather garden, collections of spring bulbs, gentians and alpine plants, and under glass, succulent plants. There are also extensive collections of trees and shrubs.

REGION 4
Alcester, Warwicks
Ragley Hall
This 17th-century home of the Seymour family lies 2 miles south-west of Alcester. There are fine gardens, and the park includes an adventure wood and country trail.

REGION 4
Alton, Staffs
Alton Towers
This ruined, early 19th-century mansion was the former home of Charles, Earl of Shrewsbury. It is set amid beautiful grounds with lakes, pools and fountains, foremost of which is the Chinese Pagoda Fountain. The grounds also contain cable cars, a boating lake, an amusement park, a planetarium a pottery and a studio.

REGION 5
Ambleside, Cumbria
Stagshaw Gardens
1 mile south of Ambleside on the A591. A magnificent garden created in mature woodland on a fell side overlooking Lake Windermere. A unique collection of species and hybrid rhododendrons, azaleas, camellias and other flowering shrubs.

REGION 6
Ardminish, Isle of Gigha, Strath
Achamore
This unique 50-acre garden of azaleas and rhododendrons was created by the late Sir James Horlick.

REGION 1
Arlington, Devon
Arlington Court
Situated 7 miles north-east of Barnstaple, off the A39. This 19th-century mansion stands in a large wooded estate with terraced gardens and a lake. The house contains fascinating collections of model ships, pewter and sea shells accumulated by the former owner, Miss Rosalie Chichester. In the stables is a large collection of horse-drawn vehicles.

REGION 1
Athelhampton, Dorset
Athelhampton
On the A35 1 mile east of Puddletown. Athelhampton is one of the finest medieval houses in southern England. Attractions include the 15th-century great hall, Tudor great chamber, fine staircase and interesting furniture. A 15th-century dovecote stands amid 10 acres of formal and landscaped gardens.

REGION 6
Balmacarra,
Highland
Balmacarra Woodland Garden
Situated in a magnificent stretch of west Highland mountainous scenery, the woodland garden includes guided walks, and there is a natural history display in the coach house.

REGION 1
Barnstaple, Devon
Marwood Hill
Here 8–10 acres include rare trees and shrubs, a rose garden, a quarry garden with alpine plants, 2 small lakes and a bog garden. Greenhouses include a camellia house and an Australian house. Plants for sale.

REGION 6
Benmore, Strath
Benmore Younger Botanic Garden
Here is woodland and garden on a grand scale, featuring conifers, rhododendrons, azaleas and many other shrubs.

REGION 4
Blicking, Norfolk
Blickling Hall
Blickling Hall is an early 17th-century red-brick mansion standing in a fine park. The state rooms include a notable collection of paintings and furnishings and there is an interesting plaster ceiling in the gallery. The formal gardens were laid out in 1793 and re-designed in 1930. Also within the park are the orangery, a temple and a crescent-shaped lake.

REGION 3
Burford, Salop
Burford House Gardens
Off the A456. These fine gardens feature trees, shrubs, clematis, herbaceous plants, roses and an 18th-century summer house. Exhibitions of paintings by local and botanical artists can be seen on the ground floor of Burford House.

REGION 2
Calne, Wilts
Bowood
2 miles west of Calne off the A4. Bowood is a magnificent Georgian house which is surrounded by pleasure grounds and gardens of over 100 acres. Attractions include a lake created by Capability Brown, Hamilton's Cascade, a grotto and a Doric temple.

REGION 1
Canford Cliffs, Dorset
Compton Acres Gardens
Rock, water, heather, Japanese, Roman, English and Italian gardens are featured here. There are fine views over Poole Harbour and the Purbeck Hills.

REGION 6
Castle Douglas, Dumf & Gall
Threave Gardens
Situated 1 mile west of Castle Douglas. These fine gardens are noted for their springtime display of over 300 varieties of daffodil. Walled garden and glasshouses.

REGION 4
Cholmondeley, Cheshire
Cholmondeley Castle Gardens
Situated 7 miles west of Nantwich on the A49. Attractions include ornamental gardens, a lakeside picnic area, rare breeds of farm animals. There is also a private chapel in the park.

REGION 6
Coldstream, Borders
Dundock Wood
From around mid May to the end of June (depending on the season) Dundock Wood is the setting for a magnificent display of rhododendrons and azaleas. It also has a large bird sanctuary and nature walks.

REGION 5
Coniston, Cumbria
Brantwood
Brantwood is situated on an unclassified road on the east side of Coniston Water, 2½ miles south-east of Coniston off the B5285. The former home of John Ruskin, it houses a memorial exhibition including his paintings and many of his personal possessions. A garden surrounds the house, which has one of the finest nature trails in the country.

REGION 3
Croft, Herefs & Worcs
Croft Castle Grounds
This restored, 14th-century mansion. situated off the B4362, is set in a 1,636-acre estate of fine oaks, beeches and avenues of Spanish chestnuts.

REGION 1
Great Torrington, Devon
Rosemoor Garden Trust
1 mile south-east of the town on the B3220. Planted in 1959, the garden specializes in species and hybrid rhododendrons, shrub roses and ornamental trees and shrubs. Unusual plants for sale.

REGION 2
Hascombe, Surrey
Winkworth Arboretum
1 mile north-west of Hascombe on the B2130. A hillside of nearly 100 acres is planted with shrubs and rare trees. Displays are best in spring and autumn. Views towards the North Downs.

REGION 4
Hathern, Leics
Whatton House Gardens
On the A6 between Hathern and Kegworth, 4½ miles north-west of Loughborough. The 25-acre gardens display flowering shrubs and have water, rose and Chinese gardens.

REGION 1
Hele, Devon
Killerton House and Gardens
5 miles north-east of Exeter on the B3185, off the B3181. The 18th-century house contains the Pauline de Bush collection of costume, shown in a series of room settings furnished in different periods ranging from the second half of the 18th century to the present day. The estate covers more than 5,000 acres including 15 acres of gardens with rare trees and shrubs.

REGION 4
Helmingham, Suffolk
Helmingham Hall Gardens
The home of Lord and Lady Tollemache, this moated house has two drawbridges which are still raised every night. The moated gardens are part of an ancient deer park which contains ornamental waterfowl, Highland cattle and over 500 red and fallow deer.

REGION 6
Inveresk, Lothian
Inveresk Lodge Garden
These new gardens feature numerous varieties of plants suitable for small gardens.

REGION 2
Isleworth, Greater London
Syon Park
Set in the grounds of Syon House, the park has 55 acres of gardens which were laid out in the mid 16th century. Reputed to be the first place where trees were planted purely for ornament, it owes much of its present beauty to Capability Brown. The Great Conservatory, built in 1820, was the first large glass and metal construction of its kind in the world, and was the inspiration for the Crystal Palace at the Great Exhibition of 1851. The 6-acre rose garden has over 12,000 roses.

REGION 2
Kew, Greater London
Kew Gardens
Magnificent trees, superb shrubs and countless flowers can all be found here, on a 300-acre site near the heart of London. There are many formal areas, but there is also an area set aside as semi-wild woodland, and it is here that birdwatchers will be able to see woodpeckers, nuthatches, tree creepers, warblers and many other birds. There are also glasshouses with rare orchids, ferns and cacti. The exotic pagoda was the work of Sir William Chambers in 1761.

REGION 6
Kilchrenan, Strath
Ardanaiseig
The gardens have azaleas, rhododendrons, rare shrubs and trees and offer magnificent views across Loch Awe.

REGION 3
Kington, Herefs & Worcs
Hergest Croft Gardens
These large gardens feature trees, shrubs, flowers and herbaceous borders, and an old-fashioned kitchen garden. There is also a wooded valley filled with rhododendrons, some 30ft tall.

REGION 1
Lanhydrock, Cornwall
Lanhydrock
This restored 17th-century mansion enjoys a richly wooded setting. There is a fine gatehouse and the picture gallery has an interesting plaster ceiling as well as 17th- to 20th-century family portraits. Paths wind through the extensive woodlands.

REGION 4
Lea, Derbys
Lea Rhododendron Gardens
These attractive woodland gardens comprising 3½ acres feature rhododendrons, azaleas and rock garden. Plant sales.

REGION 2
Liphook, Hants
Bohunt Manor
This property, which has been given to the World Wildlife Fund, includes a medium-sized woodland garden with lakeside walk, a water garden, roses, herbaceous borders, and a collection of over 100 ornamental ducks, geese and cranes.

REGION 1
Madron, Cornwall
Trengwainton Gardens
Trengwainton displays a magnificent collection of shrubs, including magnolias and rhododendrons. A walled garden contains tender and sub-tropical plants not grown elsewhere in England.

REGION 2
Mickleton, Glos
Hidcote Manor Gardens
Major Lawrence Johnston created, this series of small, formal gardens between 1908 and 1948. Various species of hedge separate each garden, and there is also a kitchen garden.

REGION 2
Mickleton, Glos
Kiftsgate Court Garden
Situated ½ mile south off the A46, adjacent to Hidcote Manor Garden. The garden has many unusual plants and shrubs, and a collection of old-fashioned roses including R Filipes Kiftsgate, the largest rose in England.

REGION 6
Minard, Strath
Crarae Gardens
Set in a Highland glen, Crarae is a woodland garden with eucalyptus, rhododendrons, rare trees and shrubs.

REGION 2
Minstead, Hants
Furzey Gardens
Amid 8 acres of peaceful glades winter and summer heathers grow, along with flowering trees and shrubs (some rare) and spring bulbs. There is also an ancient cottage (1560) now restored, where the work of 50 artists and 100 local craftsmen is displayed.

REGION 6
Muthill, Tayside
Drummond Castle Gardens
These beautiful formal gardens lie 1 mile north of Muthill.

REGION 4
Northwich, Cheshire
Arley Hall and Gardens
This early Victorian house has fine examples of plaster work, woodcarvings, pictures and furnishings. The private chapel was the work of Salvin. The gardens feature outstanding twin herbaceous borders, an unusual avenue of clipped ilex trees, walled gardens, a herb garden and scented gardens.

REGION 2
Nuneham Courtney, Oxon
Oxford University Arboretum
On the A423, just south of the village, the University Arboretum comprises 50 acres of conifers and broadleaf trees.

REGION 6
Old Dailly, Strath
Bargany Gardens
The gardens lie 4 miles north-east of Old Dailly, on the B734 from Girvan. There are woodland walks, with snowdrops, bluebells and daffodils in spring and fine displays of azaleas and rhododendrons round the lily pond in May and June. Many ornamental trees.

REGION 6
Poolewe, Highland
Inverewe Gardens
These remarkable gardens are full of interest and beauty from March to October (at their best May to early June), and contain many rare and sub-tropical plants. The magnificence is intensified by a background of majestic mountains and tranquil Loch Maree to the south.

REGION 1
Probus, Cornwall
County Demonstration Garden and Arboretum
This permanent display covers the many aspects of garden layout, plant selection, and the effect of weather conditions. Information on plant, tree and flower propagation with emphasis on choosing the right foliage, flowers etc, to suit individual requirements and environment is available. Exhibits of fruit, herbs and vegetables.

REGION 5
Rothbury, Northumb
Cragside and Country Park
Entrance for cars 2 miles north on the B6341. This Victorian house, home of the first Lord Armstrong, has the unique distinction of being the first house in the world to be lit by electricity generated by water power. The magnificent country park covers 900 acres.

REGION 2
St Albans, Herts
Royal National Rose Society's Gardens
This is the trial ground for new varieties of rose and there are over 30,000 plants in 1,650 varieties. Species roses, old-fashioned roses, modern roses and roses of the future can all be seen here.

REGION 2
Sheffield Park, E Sussex
Sheffield Park Garden
These magnificent gardens and a lake-watered park of nearly 150 acres, laid out from the 18th to the 20th century, surround one of the most beautiful houses in Sussex. Rhododendrons and azaleas (May to June) and notable trees and shrubs (autumn) can be seen.

REGION 2
Silsoe, Beds
Wrest Park Gardens
Notable 18th-century garden with formal canals that was altered by Capability Brown.

REGION 4
South Walsham, Norfolk
Fairhaven Garden Trust
The gardens contain a beech walk with spring flowers, rhododendrons, a water garden and walks beside a private Broad. The King Oak is reputed to be 900 years old. The Bird Sanctuary may be visited at certain times by arrangement with the warden.

REGION 4
Spalding, Lincs
Springfields Gardens
This unique 25-acre spring flower spectacle lies on the eastern outskirts of the town on the A151. There are more than a million bulbs; lawns, lake, glasshouses and summer rose gardens with over 12,500 rose bushes in 100 varieties.

REGION 2
Stonor, Oxon
Stonor House and Park
4 miles north-west of Henley-on-Thames on the B480. This 12th-century house, home of Lord and Lady Camoys, has been occupied by the Stonor family for the past 800 years. It contains examples of some of the earliest domestic architecture in Oxfordshire and the beautiful gardens behind the house have commanding views of the park.

REGION 2
Stourton, Wilts
Stourhead House and Gardens
This 18th-century house has many interesting paintings and Chippendale furniture. The 2,500-acre lake-watered grounds, laid out by Henry Hoare in the mid 18th century, feature contemporary garden temples, and form one of Europe's most famous layouts.

REGION 2
Taplow, Bucks
Cliveden
Cliveden House, the third to be built on this site, was designed in 1850 by Charles Barry. Its Italianate style is complemented by the beautiful grounds which overlook the River Thames. Formal gardens, dotted with Italian sculpture sweep down from the terrace at the rear, and informal areas include a lovely water garden.

REGION 1
Truro, Cornwall
Trelissick Garden
Rhododendrons and sub-tropical plants can be seen growing in this beautiful woodland park at the head of Falmouth Harbour 4 miles south of Truro. There is also a large shrub garden.

REGION 2
Wisley, Surrey
Wisley Garden
Wisley is the famous and extensive garden of the Royal Horticultural Society. It was made at the beginning of the 20th century when the planting of natural and woodland gardens, known as wild gardening, became fashionable. Today the great variety offers something of interest for every gardener.

COUNTRY PARKS

REGION 3
Cynonville, W Glam
Afan Argoed Country Park
Set in the wooded Afan valley on the A4107, the Country Park offers forest walks and trails. There are picnic areas and a Countryside Centre adjoins the parking area. Nearby is the Welsh Miners Museum where there are simulated coal faces, pit gear and miners' equipment.

REGION 4
Elvaston, Derbys
Elvaston Castle Country Park
Set in the grounds of a fine early 19th-century mansion, this 200-acre park incorporates a lake, formal gardens, a walled Old English garden and woodland. A working estate museum is housed in the lower stable yard and other attractions include a riding school and a nature trail.

REGION 6
Fairlie, Strath
Kelburn Country Centre
Lying 1 mile north-east of Fairlie, off the A78. Set on the Firth of Clyde, this is the historic estate of the Earls of Glasgow and has beautiful gardens and spectacular scenery. It offers exotic gardens, nature trails and the magnificent Kelburn Glen, complete with pools and waterfalls. Other attractions include a weaver's workshop, pony trekking and an adventure course.

REGION 1
Farway, Devon
Farway Countryside Park
Situated 1½ miles south of Farway, the park is set in 130 acres of countryside with magnificent views of the Coly Valley. Its main attractions are the rare breeds of British farm animals which are bred here, but other features include a pets' enclosure and deer enclosure.

REGION 4
Fritton, Norfolk
Fritton Lake Country Park
A lovely country park has been created on the Somerleyton estate around Fritton Lake. The landscaped grounds feature woodland and gardens and for children there is an adventure playground and pony rides. Fishing is available in season and rowing boats may be hired.

A permanent exhibition centre for the region, it includes photographs, maps, teaching aids, etc. The Reginald Farrer Trail commences here.

REGION 3
Craig y Viliau Woodlands, Powys
Interesting woodland on carboniferous limestone with small-leaved lime and whitebeams in extensive upland grassland.

REGION 3
Cwmcarn, Gwent
Scenic Forest Drive
This 7-mile drive through Ebbw Forest is maintained by the Forestry Commission. The road leads through mountainous woodland with spectacular views of the surrounding countryside and the Bristol Channel. Special features along the way include adventure play areas, forest and mountain walks and picnic places.

REGION 5
Danby, N Yorks
Danby Lodge
A former shooting lodge, Danby Lodge near Whitby offers a comprehensive information and countryside interpretation service to visitors to the North York Moors National Park. The 13 acres of riverside meadow and woodland include a brass rubbing centre, exhibition centre and children's play area. There are daily slide and film shows and guided walks.

REGION 2
Epping Forest, Essex
This extensive ancient woodland is famous for its lovely beeches, and for its ancient pollarded hornbeams.

REGION 2
Frimwell, Kent
Bedgebury National Pinetum
Situated 1½ miles north off the A21. Established by the Forestry Commission in 1925, the pinetum contains 160 acres of trees, including the most comprehensive collection of conifers in Europe, and an old hammer pond. There are also more than 100 research plots.

REGION 3
Garwnant Forest Centre, M Glam
5 miles north of Merthyr Tydfil off the A470. Garwnant Forest Centre provides information about, and an exhibition featuring the forests in, the Brecon Beacons. Forest walks.

REGION 6
Glencoe, Highland
Glen Coe Visitor Centre
Situated at the north end of Glen Coe, the centre is close to the scene of the 1692 massacre. A ranger-naturalist service is available.

REGION 6
Kilmun, Strath
Kilmun Arboretum and Forest Plots
A large collection of conifer and broad-leaved tree species are planted here in plots and specimen groups.

REGION 2
Horndean, Hants
Queen Elizabeth Country Park
Under the joint management of the Forestry Commission and Hampshire County Council, the park is situated on the A3 to the south of Petersfield on Gravel Hill. The 1,400 acres of downland and forest include several marked trails of various lengths and the Butser Ancient Farm, a working reconstruction of an Iron Age farm. This is run along the same lines as it would have been some 2,300 years ago. Even the farm animals are the nearest surviving breeds to Iron Age species – Exmoor ponies, Dexter cattle and Soay sheep. A shepherd's hut forms part of a permanent exhibition on sheep farming which includes displays of shearing and sheepdog trials.

REGION 6
Kirkoswald, Strath
Culzean Country Park
This magnificent park covers 560 acres, and includes an 18th-century walled garden, a camellia house, an orangery, swan pond and an aviary. A reception and interpretation centre is housed in the former home farm buildings.

REGION 3
Margam, W Glam
Margam Country Park
Landscaped gardens, a deer park and a rhododendron avenue form just a part of this 800-acre park. Various ruined buildings, including the chapter house of Margam Abbey, a 16th-century mansion and a castle, can be seen, but the most splendid is the orangery – the largest of its kind in Britain. Other attractions include pony trekking, waymarked walks, archery competitions, an adventure playground, boating and the Coach House Theatre.

REGION 4
Newton Lindford, Leics
Bradgate Park and Swithland Woods
A country park covering 850 acres has been created from Bradgate Park and nearby Swithland Woods. The former surrounds the ruins of 16th-century Bradgate House and contains large herds of deer. Nature trails are another feature of the Park.

WOODLANDS, NATIONAL PARK AND VISITOR CENTRES

REGION 6
Argyll Forest Park, Strath
Managed by the Forestry Commission, this extensive forest park covers rugged hillsides reaching to the western shores of Loch Long. Good walks and recreational facilities.

REGION 6
Glen More Forest Park, Highland
This Forestry Commission land near Aviemore has a large coverage of spruce plantation with some Scots pine. Forest walks and nature observation posts.

REGION 6
Ben Lawers, Tayside
Mountain Visitor Centre
The centre stands on the slopes of Ben Lawers, a mountain noted for its birdlife and alpine flora. At 3,984ft, it is the region's highest mountain. The Centre includes an exhibition and self-guided or guided trails.

REGION 2
Burnham Beeches, Bucks
This is a splendid example of extensive beechwood interspersed with pedunculate oak, birch and holly on acidic gravels. An interesting epiphytic flora can be seen.

REGION 4
Cannock Chase, Staffs
Sessile oak, birch and alder grow here among the heathland and valley bog and fen. Forestry Commission areas offer good public access.

REGION 4
Charnwood Forest, Leics
Fragmented areas of once extensive pedunculate and sessile oak woodlands grow here where there once was extensive coverage. Public access at Bradgate Park and Beacon Hill.

The park was laid out in 1930 by the Forestry Commission and it now extends 100 acres over a hillside overlooking Holy Loch.

REGION 1
Glentrool Forest Park, Dumf & Gall
Good forest walks can be taken through this large Forestry Commission plantation which includes Loch Trool and 16 other lochs. Arboretum at Kinoughtree.

REGION 5
Grassington, N Yorks
National Park Centre
The centre features a display on conservation and the management of the National Park authority.

REGION 5
Grizedale, Cumbria
Visitor and Wildlife Centre
This centre is operated by the Forestry Commission in Grizedale Forest and it includes a Forest Information Centre and a deer museum with large-scale photographic dioramas. Millwood Forest nature trail, as well as other walks, are nearby. A theatre in the forest stages various events from natural history programmes to jazz, folk and classical music concerts.

REGION 5
Grizedale Forest, Cumbria
Moorland with extensive conifer plantations managed by the Forestry Commission. Some broadleaved and mixed woodlands. Additional habitats have been created for wildlife and there is good public access with guides and trails.

REGION 5
Hawes, N Yorks
National Park Centre
An exhibition which relates the social and economic history of the area as part of a national park.

REGION 5
Kielder Forest Park, Northumb
This large forest area is mainly conifer (Forestry Commission) growing among open moorland. Public access with guides and trails.

REGION 3
Maesgwm, Gwynedd
Forest Information Centre
An interpretative centre that illustrates the forest's role in the community from its place in the landscape to its use in industry and as a habitat for wildlife. The centre includes a display of machinery from local gold mines.

REGION 5
Malham, N Yorks
Yorkshire Dales National Park Centre
The Malham area is covered by this permanent interpretation centre which houses books, maps, teaching aids and displays.

REGION 5
Malham Woods, N Yorks
These rich woodlands on the carboniferous limestone of Upper Wharfedale contain a wealth of ground flora, including many local species. Good public access within the National Park.

REGION 2
New Forest, Hants
Managed by the Forestry Commission, this one-time royal hunting forest comprises mixed oak and beech woodland with bog and heathland habitats. There are also large areas of coniferous plantations. Extremely popular leisure area, with camp and picnic sites, forest walks and nature trails.

REGION 6
Queen's View, Tayside
Tummel Forest Centre
Queen Victoria's favourite scene in Scotland. Exhibits at the centre record the changes in the magnificent Tummel valley since the Queen's visit in 1866. Included are a diorama and a model of a Highland clachan in the forest, which has recently been excavated and partly restored. Slides and sound show. Information desk. Forest walks and picnic areas. Regular access.

REGION 6
Rothiemurchas Forest, Highland
This is the largest remaining semi-natural Scots pine forest. It is of open structure with a rich shrub layer, including juniper.

REGION 2
Savernake Forest, Wilts
Formerly an old deer park, this extensive woodland is planted with oak and larch. Many ancient oaks and beeches can still be seen. Good birdwatching site with public access and nature trail.

REGION 5
Sedbergh, Cumbria
National Park Centre
A visitor centre for Sedbergh and the surrounding area.

REGION 3
Snowdonia Forest Park, Gwynedd
Conifer plantations managed by the Forestry Commission. There are also streams, waterfalls and an arboretum. There are many forest walks in the area, and the Gwydyr Forest Walk is especially for the disabled.

REGION 5
Windermere, Cumbria
Lake District National Park Centre
The centre is housed in a 19th-century house amid 32 acres of gardens and woodland on the eastern shore of Lake Windermere. Items of interest include audio-visual displays, films and an information room. Lake launch trips and garden tours take place each summer and there are special family events during the school holidays.

REGION 2
Westonbirt, Glos
Westonbirt Arboretum
Part of a 600-acre Forestry Commission estate, the arboretum includes one of the finest collections of trees in Europe. Several rare specimens are nurtured here and the variety of conifers, maples and oaks is particularly noteworthy.

WILDLIFE COLLECTIONS

REGION 1
Abbotsbury, Dorset
Abbotsbury Swannery
Over 500 swans nest and breed at this famous swannery which was established by the monks of Abbotsbury in the 14th century. It is also the home or port of call for a great many species of other wild birds. These include various species of duck and many waders, as well as plovers, terns, owls and smaller birds like wagtails.

REGION 6
Ardfern, Strath
Argyll Wildlife Centre
The centre enjoys a natural setting on a small hill within an area of old Caledonian oak woodland and marshland. A showcase of mammals, birds, trees and plants, formerly or currently native to Scotland. The primary objectives here are education and conservation.

REGION 6
Barcaldine, Strath
Sea Life Centre
Situated at Loch Creran, the Centre has the largest collection of native marine life in Britain and species of marine creatures – ranging from sea anemones, through various kinds of fish, to seals – can be studied at close quarters. To provide a better understanding of underwater life two artificial rock pools have been created: one enables visitors to actually pick up and touch the inhabitants, and the other shows the effect strong tidal waves have on the life of the pool.

REGION 2
Basildon, Berks
Child Beale Wildlife Trust
Rare sheep and Highland cattle are among the animals seen here. Other attractions include riverside walks and lakes with ornamental pheasants, peacocks, wildfowl, flamingoes and cranes.

REGION 2
Berwick, E Sussex
Drusillas Zoo Park
Rare breeds of British cattle are the main attraction at this centre for the Rare Breeds Survival Trust, although sheep and poultry can also be seen. Another feature is the exhibition of Sussex wagons, ox harness and farm implements.

REGION 4
Birmingham, W Midlands
Birmingham Nature Centre
Located at the south-west entrance to Cannon Hill Park, opposite Pebble Mill Road. Living animals of the British Isles and Europe are on show here in both indoor and outdoor enclosures. Conditions have been created to resemble natural habitats, and to attract wild birds and butterflies etc, thus forming a miniature wildlife park.

REGION 6
Caerlaverock, Dumf & Gall
Wildfowl Trust
Outstanding hide facilities, observation towers and an observatory provide impressive views of the flocks of barnacle and pink-footed geese, whooper and Bewick swans, and of the numerous species of duck that winter here.

REGION 3
Cardigan, Dyfed
Cardigan Wildlife Park
The entrance to the park is near Cilgerran village, off the A478. The animals of Wales, past and present, are a major feature of Cardigan Wildlife Park. They can be seen with other European animals in an unusually diverse area of natural habitats covering 250 acres. Other attractions include nature trails, a wildlife sanctuary and demonstrations of coracle fishing.

REGION 5
Chillingham, Northumb
Chillingham Wild Cattle
A park in the grounds of Chillingham Castle (which is not open to the public) contains a herd of some 50 white cattle. They are believed to be descendants of Britain's native wild cattle, and have escaped cross breeding because they have been isolated in the park for hundreds of years.

REGION 1
Over Compton, Dorset
Worldwide Butterflies Ltd and Lullingstone Silk Farm
Compton House, near Sherborne, is the home of a fascinating butterfly farm. The collections, which are from all over the world, are displayed in natural jungle habitat and a tropical palm house. It is also the home of the silk farm which produced the silk for the last two coronations and for the Queen's wedding dress.

REGION 1
Cricket St Thomas, Somerset
Wildlife Park and Country Life Museum
This historic and beautiful park, with 9 lakes, is the setting for a fascinating collection of wild animals and birds, including a tropical walk-through aviary. It is also the home of the National Horse Centre.

REGION 6
Dunkeld, Tayside
Loch of Lowes Wildlife Reserve
As well as a variety of wildlife, the reserve has an observation hide where visitors can watch great crested grebes and other waterfowl in their natural surroundings. Exhibition and slide programme in visitor centre.

REGION 4
Earsham, Suffolk
Otter Trust
This 23-acre site holds the world's largest collection of captive otters. They are kept in semi-natural conditions and bred for release into the wild and for research purposes. The main aim of the Trust is to help save the world's otters from extinction.

REGION 1
Gweek, Cornwall
Gweek Seal Sanctuary
There are always plenty of seals to see at this sanctuary for these 'orphans of the sea' washed up on the Cornish coast. It comprises a hospital and five pools.

REGION 6
Kincraig, Highland
Highland Wildlife Park
This park concentrates on native animals of Scotland past and present, including wolves, bears, reindeer, wildcats and European bison.

REGION 5
Martin Mere, Lancs
Martin Mere Wildfowl Trust
Martin Mere's collection of waterfowl is one of the most comprehensive in the world. The 50-acre waterfowl garden contains several European species and various exotic endangered birds such as Hawaiian Duck and Layson Teal. A large lake and marshland area next door is popular with visiting waders and hundreds of resident and visiting geese and snipe can be seen.

REGION 4
Neath, W Glam
Penscynor Wildlife Park
A bird collection, including flamingoes and penguins forms the backbone to this wildlife park and there is a walk-through aviary and a tropical bird house. Several mammals can also be seen and there is a small aquarium.

REGION 2
Newent, Glos
Birds of Prey Conservation and Falconry Centre
1 mile south-west of Newent on an unclassified road to Clifford's Mesne. The centre has one of the largest collections of birds of prey in the world. All the trained birds may be seen in the Hawk Walk and there is also a museum and a flying ground where birds are flown daily. The breeding aviaries and brooder room can be visited.

REGION 4
Peakirk, Cambs
Peakirk Wildfowl Trust
Over 100 different species of swans, ducks and geese can be seen in this attractive water garden. There are many rare and unusual waterfowl, including a magnificent flock of Chilean flamingoes.

REGION 2
Slimbridge, Glos
Slimbridge Wildfowl Trust
Off the A38 and M5, junction 13. Founded by, and under the direction of, Sir Peter Scott, Slimbridge probably has the most important collection of captive and fully winged migrant waterfowl in the world. First-class viewing facilities are available and there are permanent exhibitions and a tropical house.

REGION 2
Stagsden, Beds
Stagsden Bird Gardens
A breeding centre for rare pheasants, waterfowl and old breeds of poultry and other birds.

REGION 6
Torridon, Highland
Trust Visitor Centre
Standing amid some of Scotland's finest scenery, the centre is situated at the junction of the A896 and the Diabeg road. There are audio-visual presentations on wildlife and, at nearby Mains, a static display on the life of the red deer. There is also a collection of live animals.

REGION 5
Washington, Tyne & Wear
Washington Wildfowl Trust
A comprehensive collection of the world's waterfowl can be seen in this 103-acre waterfowl park on the banks of the River Wear. There are public hides and a visitor centre. Bookshop and Lecture Theatre.

REGION 4
Welney, Norfolk
Welney Wildfowl Trust
This 800-acre wildfowl refuge on the Ouse Washes is winter home to vast numbers of migratory swans, geese and ducks. There is a spacious observatory, a series of hides and, in winter, a floodlit lagoon containing hundreds of Bewick swans.

REGION 2
Weyhill, Hants
The Hawk Conservancy, Weyhill Wildlife Park
This is a specialist collection of birds of prey, including hawks, falcons, eagles, owls and vultures. Birds are flown daily, weather permitting.

CAVERNS AND GORGES

REGION 3
Abercrave, Powys
Dan-yr-Ogof and Cathedral Showcaves
Situated 3 miles north of Abercrave on the A4067. This is the biggest show cave complex in Western Europe and boasts some of the largest stalactites and stalagmites in the country. Visitors are given guided tours of the passages.

REGION 1
Avon Gorge, Avon
Famous to botanists, this spectacular gorge has been carved by the River Avon, out of the limestone at Bristol. Partly National Nature Reserve, the habitat includes woodland, scrub and limestone cliffs.

REGION 4
Buxton, Derbys
Buxton Country Park and Pooles Cavern
Pooles Cavern, a natural limestone cave, forms the centrepiece of the 100-acre wooded country park. An interpretative centre, featuring displays and side shows, illustrates the history of the cave and the surrounding area.

REGION 4
Castleton, Derbys
Blue-John Cavern and Mine
The finest of the Derbyshire caves, the Blue-John Cavern is ⅓-mile long with chambers 200ft high. It is named after the veins of rare Blue John rock – prized since Roman times – that are found there.

REGION 4
Castleton, Derbys
Peak Cavern
This natural limestone cave is one of the most spectacular in the district. A ½-mile underground walk is illuminated to reveal many grotesque natural shapes. Ropes have been made at the entrance to the cave for over 500 years.

REGION 4
Castleton, Derbys
Speedwell Cavern
The main attraction in this floodlit cavern is the illuminated canal leading to the bottomless pit which can only be reached by boats.

REGION 1
Cheddar, Somerset
Cheddar Caves and Museum
These are probably the finest show caves in Britain. They are well-lit with magnificent stalactite and stalagmite formations, in the two main caves – Gough's and Cox's. The man-made Waterfall Grotto and a steep flight of steps, known as Jacob's Ladder, leading up to the top of the gorge, are additional attractions.

A museum is situated on The Cliffs and it includes exhibits on archaeology and zoology. Flint and bone implements dating from the Ice Age, which were found in Gough's Cave, are preserved here.

REGION 1
Cheddar Gorge, Somerset
A famous feature of the Somerset landscape, this impressive dry gorge winds down through the limestone in the Mendip Hills. Rare flora grows on the limestone screes and rocks.

REGION 1
Ebbor Gorge, Somerset
The carboniferous limestone supports a fine example of ash woodland with rich ground flora and lovely whitebeams. Limited access. Nature Conservancy Council nature trail in National Nature Reserve.

REGION 1
Lydford, Devon
Lydford Gorge
The gorge can be found 8 miles north of Tavistock, on an unclassified road. Scooped into a succession of potholes by the River Lyd, the gorge emerges into a steep, oak-wooded valley and is joined by another stream at the 90ft-high White Lady waterfall. The steep valley woodlands which enclose the gorge are exceptionally rich in wild flowers and ferns.

COAST AND CLIFFS

REGION 5
Bardsea Country Park, Cumbria
2 miles south of Ulverston on the A5087. The coastal strip comprises shingle and mudflats with 60 acres of oak wood, footpaths and a picnic area. Good bird-watching areas.

REGION 1
Brownsea Island, Dorset
Situated in Poole Harbour, the island can be reached by ferry from Poole Quay and Sandbanks. This National Trust property includes two lakes, marshland, a nature reserve and a beach. The habitat is mainly heath and woodland and red squirrels can be seen. There is also a heronry, ternery, a public hide and an information centre.

REGION 6
Caerlaverock, Dumf & Gall
7 miles south of Dumfries. A National Nature Reserve with saltmarsh and sandy foreshore. The area is managed as a refuge for wildfowl; barnacle, pink-footed and greylag geese can be spotted in winter.

REGION 6
Caithness Coast, Highland
Large colonies of breeding seabirds gather along this impressive stretch of coastline. There is superb cliff scenery at Duncansby Head.

REGION 1
Chapel Porth, Cornwall
A National Trust nature trail starts at the car park 2 miles west of St Agnes village. Access off the B3277 road to St Agnes. The trail passes through the Chapel Porth valley, alongside a stream and over the clifftops. There is an area of heathland, with many plants and animals of heathland habitats. Seals can sometimes be seen from the cliffs.

REGION 1
Chesil Beach, Dorset
Access via the B1357 from Abbotsbury or the A354 from Portland. In winter many ducks can be seen in the Fleet, a tidal lagoon enclosed by this, one of Britain's largest shingle beaches. Shingle flora includes sea pea, sea holly and sea kale.

REGION 6
Culbin Sands, Grampian
6 miles east of Nairn. Extensive sand dunes, shingle and afforested areas. Flats and salt marsh, enclosed by sand bars, provide feeding grounds for many birds.

REGION 1
Dawlish Warren, Devon
Situated 9 miles south-east of Exeter, off the A379. This double sand spit across the Exe estuary is a local nature reserve with a public bird-watching hide. Among the birds that can be seen are oystercatchers, redshanks and grey plovers.

REGION 5
Flamborough Head and Bampton Cliffs, Humberside
5 miles north-east of Bridlington. The chalk cliffs here rise an impressive 300ft sheer from the sea. Colonies of nesting birds can be seen here in their thousands, including gannets, guillemots, kittiwakes and puffins.

REGION 1
Isles of Scilly, Cornwall
The Isles of Scilly comprise a group of between 200 and 300 small islands and rocks of the same granite formation as the mainland. Unusual flora and fauna can be found here, due to the exceptionally mild climate.

REGION 1
Kynance Cove, Cornwall
Off the A3083 via toll road. Designated a Site of Special Scientific Interest and jointly controlled by the National Trust and Cornwall Naturalists' Trust, the Cove has a multi-coloured serpentine cliff line, broken by sandy bays and caves. The very rich flora of this area is given its diversity by the variety of soil types; the heathland flora is unique. The impressive rock formations can be dangerous to explore.

REGION 1
Land's End, Cornwall
9 miles south-west of Penzance, at the end of the A30. The exposed granite cliffs of this area are rich in colourful lichens and other coastal flora such as sea pink, sea carrot and rock samphire.

REGION 1
Lundy Island, Devon
This tiny granite island lies in the Bristol Channel, and can be reached by steamer from Ilfracombe. Puffins and other seabirds breed in large numbers on cliffs around the coastline.

REGION 5
Lytham St Annes, Lancs
On the A584 between Lytham St Annes and Blackpool. A local nature reserve of dunes which is home to many common birds and a selection of moths and butterflies. Plant-life includes kidney vetch, rest-harrow and marsh orchid.

REGION 3
Newborough Warren, Anglesey
Off the A4080 9 miles west of Menai Bridge. One of the largest dune systems on Britain's western coastline, Newborough Warren covers an area of more than 1,500 acres. The varied habitats range from bare sand to grassland.

REGION 4
North Norfolk Coast
The constructive action of the sea is well illustrated along the section of coast between Weybourne and Hunstanton. Marshes, dunes and spits, in all stages of formation, can be seen.

REGION 6
North Rona and Sula Sgeir
These two remote islands are 43 miles from Cape Wrath at the tip of northern Scotland. They offer ideal breedng conditions, for gannets on Sula, and grey seals on North Rona.

REGION 1
Poole Harbour, Dorset
Sand and shingle beaches enclose this land-locked harbour. Saltmarsh and estuarine habitats; birdlife includes grebes, waders and ducks. Part of the harbour is a National Nature Reserve.

REGION 5
St Bees Head, Cumbria
Access via public footpath from the villages of St Bees and Sandwith. This is a property of the Royal Society for the Protection of Birds. April to August are the best months for spotting seabirds on the sandstone cliffs. There are breeding colonies of fulmars, guillemots, razorbills and puffins.

REGION 3
St David's Head, Dyfed
North-west of St Davids off the B4583. The steep cliffs are mainly composed of acidic rock, and these give way to heathland with grassland rich in flora. Breeding birds include buzzards, ravens and choughs.

REGION 6
South Ardnamurchan Coast, Highland
The most westerly point on the Scottish mainland, South Ardnamurchan has a narrow rock-strewn shoreline bordered by grassy cliff terraces and wooded slopes. The mild climate produces a rich flora.

REGION 3
Tenby Peninsula, Dyfed
Carboniferous limestone cliffs with arches, caves and stacks characterize the peninsula's coastline. Stackpole Head is especially rich in plant life. The Pembrokeshire Coast Long Distance Path can be followed along the coast from Tenby to Bosherston.

REGION 1
The Lizard, Cornwall
Part National Nature Reserve, the Lizard is formed from serpentine, a rock seldom found in this country. The rich and varied flora includes the rare Cornish heath, a species of heather.

REGION 2
The Naze, Essex
Near Walton-on-the-Naze, off the B1034. A popular bird-watching site, the Naze comprises shingle, saltmarsh and mudflats with rich flora and birdlife.

REGION 4
The Wash, Lincs
Waders and wildfowl can be seen in large numbers along the mudflats and saltmarshes, and also on the farmland and reclaimed pastures close to the shores of the Wash. Excellent birdwatching area with many uncommon species present. Summertime brings a splendid array of flowering saltmarsh plants.

FENS AND MARSHLAND

REGION 6
Aber Bogs, Strath
10 miles north of Glasgow on the A811. The bogs are a mixture of swamp and scrubland with open pools located on the southern part of the Loch Lomond marshes, where the River Endrick joins the loch. Wetland plants and bird life.

REGION 6
Caerlaverock, Dumf & Gall
7 miles south of Dumfries on the B725. This National Nature Reserve on the Scottish shore of the Solway Firth is an extensive salt marsh. Many wildfowl can be seen here in winter, particularly barnacle geese. Also a breeding ground of the rare natterjack toad.

REGION 3
Cors Tregaron, Dyfed
Situated north of the little town of Tregaron, this is a fine example of one of the few raised bogs in England and Wales which is still actively growing. The very rare red kite can sometimes be seen here.

REGION 6
Loch Irish and Irish Marshes, Highland
12 miles south-west of Aviemore, between the B970 and the A9 from Kingussie to Kincraig. Part of this 2,470-acre marsh and bogland is a RSPB reserve with a great variety of over-wintering ducks and waders. Wetlands also rich in plant life.

REGION 5
Malham Tarn and Moss, N Yorks
6 miles east of Settle. This raised bog and complex fen system covers one end of an unusually calcium-rich upland tarn.

REGION 1
Marazion Marsh, Cornwall
3½ miles east of Penzance off the A394. This marsh with its shallow pools and reed beds lies across the

causeway from St Michael's Mount. It is a popular birdwatching area; spring and autumn sees waders on passage while large numbers of divers and grebes gather in winter. Marine life includes blennies, Cornish sucker fish and molluscs.

REGION 2
New Forest Valley Bogs, Hants
Many valley bogs have formed in the sands and gravels of the New Forest. These are often found in heathland areas. Dragonflies and damselflies are specialities of such areas.

REGION 4
Norfolk Broads, Norfolk
Now a popular recreation ground, the Norfolk Broads were formed as a result of extensive peat digging during medieval times. Habitats range from unspoilt woodland and gentle rolling grassland to reed-fringed waters. The Broadland Conservation Centre is a thatched building which floats on pontoons at its mooring between the Malthouse Broads and Ranworth. It houses exhibitions on the Broads' history and natural history. Breeding ground of the rare and exotic swallowtail butterfly. Wildlife is plentiful with many unusual species inhabiting the woods, reedbeds and marshland.

REGION 2
North Kent Marshes, Kent
Low-lying mudflats, salt marshes and rough grazing marshland, occupying the Medway and Swale estuaries. Large numbers of waders and wildfowl winter here.

REGION 2
Slimbridge, Glos
A wintering area for many wildfowl, this expanse of salt marsh is a National Wildfowl Refuge managed by the Wildfowl Trust. See also *Wildlife Collections p. 110.*

REGION 4
Wicken Fen, Cambs
Access by permit only. Apply to the Warden. Situated 8 miles south of Ely on the A10, then A1123. A National Trust nature reserve, this fenland area includes scrubland and reedbeds and is rich in plants, insects and birdlife.

REGION 2
Woodham Fen, Essex
Off B1012 near Woodham Ferrers. This nature reserve comprises part freshwater marsh, part salt marsh. The area is rich in flora and insect life and there is a variety of marshland birds and waders.

REGION 4
Woodwalton Fen, Cambs
Access is by permit only to this National Nature Reserve. Varied habitat includes birch wood, damp woodland, fen and open water in meres and dykes. The area has a large variety of plant species and is also the breeding ground for a number of rare insects.

HEATHS AND MOORLANDS

REGION 1
Bodmin Moor, Cornwall
Lies 3½ miles west of Launceston, crossed by the A30. This extensive upland moor is a Site of Special Scientific Interest. A variety of mosses and lichens grow around the tors. Plant life also includes eyebright, pennywort and sundew, and butterwort can be found in the wetter areas.

REGION 4
Breck heathlands, Norfolk & Suffolk
The Brecklands support a unique flora. Although many of the habitats are now destroyed, typical Breckland scenery and flora can still be seen in some areas. Lakenheath Warren, Foxhole Heath and Weeting Heath are all National Nature Reserves with habitats ranging from heather-covered heath, through various types of grassland to calcareous regions. Open landscapes of sand and flint are a feature. Rare birds, plants and insects can be seen. Restricted access. Heathland areas can be seen at West Stow Country Park, 5 miles north-west of Bury St Edmunds.

REGION 5
Brimham, N Yorks
Brimham Rocks
These curiously-shaped rocks stand on heathery moorland at a height of 950ft and lie off the B6265. Victorian guide-books described them as 'a place wrecked with grim and hideous forms defying all description and definition.' However, a few words of description can be obtained from the old shooting lodge which has been converted into an information centre.

REGION 4
Cavenham Heath, Suffolk
8 miles north-west of Bury St Edmunds, off the A1101 near Icklingham. This nature reserve spans fens, woodland and heath. Wildlife includes roe deer and adders and there are many birds. Typical heathland flora flourishes here.

REGION 2
Chobham Common, Surrey
An area of dry heathland close to Woking, Chobham Common is rich in bird and insect life. There are a number of damp valleys in which rare plants can be found.

REGION 1
Dartmoor, Devon
Habitat is largely heather moor and rough grazing, with blanket peat and several valley bogs. The rounded granite hills rise to a height of 1,800 feet at Yes Tor.

REGION 1
Exmoor, Somerset & Devon
A good proportion of Exmoor is heather moor with rough grassland in the valleys. The red sandstone hills rise to 1,705 feet at Dunkery Beacon.

REGION 5
Forest of Bowland, Lancs
A region of wild moorland fells, designated an Area of Outstanding Natural Beauty and offering some of the roughest and most remote walking in the county. Birdlife is plentiful and includes ring ouzel, merlin and short-eared owl. Black grouse can be seen on the moorland edges.

REGION 6
Mainland Orkney
There are two moorland RSPB reserves here, namely Hobbister and the Dale of Coltasgarth. Both are good sites for watching birds of prey such as the skua and hen harrier. Cliff-nesting sea birds can be seen at another RSPB reserve at Marwick Head.

REGION 2
New Forest Heathlands, Hants
The vast areas of heathland within the New Forest are of international importance for their insects, reptiles, plants and birds. Conditions vary from wet to dry heath and valley mire. Open access over much of the area.

REGION 5
North Yorkshire Moors, N Yorks
The most easterly of the uplands, the North Yorkshire Moors form a smooth plateau comprising mainly heather moor rising to a height of 1,400 feet.

REGION 1
Purbeck Heath, Dorset
Including Studland Heath, Hartland Moor and Arne Heath. This extensive area of lowland heathland is of national importance for its wildlife. There are three National Nature Reserves and an RSPB reserve. Habitat also includes open water and valley mire.

REGION 6
Rannoch Moor, Tayside
A large area of upland peat bogs, moorland and lochans rich in bog plants and insect life. The moor is edged by the remains of a pinewood and surrounded by the Grampian Mountains.

LAKES, LOCHS AND TARNS

REGION 5
Buttermere, Cumbria
This glacial valley lake lies in the heart of the Lake District National Park. It is surrounded by a varied landscape ranging from rugged crags to pastoral land.

REGION 5
Esthwaite Water, Cumbria
Access is restricted, but there are fine views from the B5285 and Water Side Woods on the east shore. The most productive of all the lakes in the Lake District, its nutrient-rich water is enjoyed by water lilies, water lobelia, water milfoils and some rare pondweeds. Birdlife found here includes the great crested and little grebe and the greylag goose. Also part of the Lake District National Park.

REGION 4
Grafham Water, Cambs
6½ miles north of St Neots, off the B661. Access by public footpath. The damming of a shallow valley resulted in this lowland reservoir which is also used as a recreational site. One of the best places in England for watching water birds.

REGION 3
Lake Vyrnwy, Powys
This reservoir in the Berwyn mountains was formed by the damming of the upper valley of the River Vyrnwy. Diving ducks and grebes can be seen on the open water, while birds such as sandpipers hunt for food in the shallows.

REGION 5
Lake Windermere, Cumbria
At 10 miles long by 1 mile wide, Lake Windermere is the largest lake in England. Its well-wooded shores attract nesting tits and warblers. Waterbirds include mallard, tufted duck, teal, pochard and shelduck. Part of the Lake District National Park.

REGION 6
Loch Lomond, Strath
The largest lake in Great Britain, Loch Lomond stretches for 24 miles and its width varies between ¾ mile and 5 miles. There are 30 islands on the loch, the most significant being Inchmurrin, on which a ruined castle stands. A variety of habitats support a good cross-section of Britain's wildlife.

REGION 3
Thames Valley Reservoirs
Used mainly for short-term storage of Thames water prior to treatment, these reservoirs are built with a raised embankment, keeping the water level above that of the surrounding land. They are especially rich in wildfowl during the winter months.

REGION 5
Wastwater, Cumbria
The deepest of the Lake District lakes, Wastwater is very unproductive. The water which enters the lake runs off scree and bare rocks and has therefore a poor mineral content.

REGION 3
White Mere, Salop
Formed within a small kettle hole, White Mere is one of many similar formations in the area. Such meres are usually very rich in wildlife, and are exciting places to look for flowers and plants.

MEADOWS AND DOWNS

REGION 1
Brean Down, Somerset
2 miles south of Weston-super-Mare. This interesting limestone headland forms the south arm of Weston Bay. The down comprises steep grassland slopes with rocky outcrops which shelter a rich plant life, including many rare species. A resting place for migrating birds crossing the Bristol Channel.

REGION 2
Compton Down, Isle of Wight
These chalky downs on the south side of the island are close to the sea and so the plant life is influenced by maritime conditions. Good for insect life, especially butterflies.

REGION 4
Devil's Ditch, Cambs
Intersected by the A45 south-west of Newmarket. The Devil's Ditch is an impressive linear earthwork which dates from between 350 and 700 AD and measures about 8 miles in length. It crosses an area of fine grassland and belongs to the Cambridgeshire and Ely Naturalists' Trust.

REGION 1
Lizard Downs, Cornwall
Coastal and heathland habitats on the distinctive serpentine rock of the Lizard Peninsula. Many rare plants.

REGION 4
Ouse Washes, Cambs & Norfolk
This area of meadow grassland lies between the parallel Old and New Bedford rivers and it is used in winter for flood storage. An interesting variety of grassland and aquatic plants grow here but the washes' main attraction is the birdlife. In winter there are large concentrations of wildfowl and some rare breeding species in summer.

REGION 2
Rodborough Common, Glos
An area of commonland with a variety of habitats including Cotswold grasslands. Several interesting flowers can be seen growing on the limestone.

REGION 1
Somerset Levels, Somerset
This low-lying flatland in central Somerset covers an area of approximately 165 square miles and is one of the most important wetland regions in the south. Meadowland flora is rich in certain sections and birdlife includes Bewick swans, white-fronted geese and other wintering waders and wildfowl. Spring and early summer brings breeding snipe, redshank, yellow wagtail, curlew and lapwing.

REGION 5
Upper Teesdale, N Yorks
The upper reaches of these hay meadows are famous for their flora. Characteristic northern species are found in the dales.

MOUNTAINS

REGION 6
Ben Lawers, Tayside
4 miles north-east of Killin, on the A827. A National Nature Reserve, 3,984ft-high Ben Lawers mountain and its surrounding moorland habitat is an area famous for arctic-alpine flora. The reserve includes a visitor centre, with historical and geological displays, and a nature trail with guided walks in summer.

REGION 6
Beinn Eighe, Highland
This 3,474ft-high mountain is rich in mountain flora with moss beds and dwarf heath. It has a pine wood at its base.

REGION 6
Cairngorms, Highland
Extensive granite plateau reaching a height of 4,300ft. These mountains have the most 'arctic' conditions in Britain. Plant life is specially adapted to growing in regions of long snow lie. Habitats include mountain heath and moorland, pine woodland and birch scrub bogs. Red deer and wildcat are natives of this region and birdlife includes the golden eagle, ptarmigan and snow bunting.

REGION 3
Cambrian Mountains, Mid Wales
Peat and heather moor culminating in the great, wet dome of Plynlimon. Mainly moorland, but there are areas of woodland and some beautiful river valleys. The red kite, one of Britain's rarest birds, breeds in a few places in this remote and wild area.

REGION 5
Cheviots, Northumb & Borders
Partly within the Northumberland National Park, the Cheviots are rounded volcanic rocks covered with heather moorland, with upland grassland on the lower slopes.

REGION 6
Grampian Mountains, Grampian
Many peaks exceed 3,000ft in this the main mountain range of the central Highlands. There are several nature reserves within its bounds, and a rich mountain vegetation.

REGION 5
Lake District, Cumbria
The steep glacial peaks rise to around 3,000 ft, with deep lakes and valleys. The area is rich in arctic/alpine vegetation and there are lovely deciduous woodlands cloaking many of the valley sides.

REGION 4
Peak District, Derbys
These millstone grit hills comprise extensive blanket peat, partly eroded, with cotton grass. The National Park contains nature reserves and nature trails.

REGION 3
Snowdonia, Gwynedd
The northern end of the Cambrians' high rocky peaks, Snowdonia has been much eroded by glaciation and is rich in mountain vegetation. The majestic summit of the Snowdon range, Yr Wyddfa, reaches 3,560ft. The National Park includes nature trails and nature reserves.

REGION 6
The Merrick, Dumf & Gall
12 miles off the A714, north of Newton Stewart near Loch Trool. At 2,764ft, the Merrick is the highest mountain in the southern uplands of Scotland. Moorland flora and birdlife on the lower slopes give way to upland and mountain species, including the alpine saw-wort and starry saxifrage, and the raven and peregrine falcon. Wild animals include red deer and feral goats.

RIVERS AND ESTUARIES

REGION 1
Camel Estuary, Cornwall
Situated 6 miles north-west of Bodmin on Cornwall's north coast, this estuary has tidal marshes and sand dunes which support a rich flora. Birdlife includes white-fronted geese, grebes and waders of many kinds.

REGION 1
Exe Estuary, Devon
This estuary is a Site of Special Scientific Interest with large areas of mud and sand at low tide. Part of the estuary is a bird sanctuary and many species can be seen.

REGION 1
Fal Estuary, Cornwall
Backed by a salt marsh, this deep estuary with inter-tidal flats has been designated a Site of Special Scientific Interest.

REGION 5
Ribble Estuary, Lancs
Among the most common of the birds seen along this area of extensive salt marsh and sandflats is the pink-footed goose which winters here in large numbers. There are also numerous waders including knot and dunlin. There are footpaths on either bank.

REGION 2
River Avon, Wilts
This lovely river rises from the chalk of Salisbury Plain. Marshes and water meadows can be found along the lower reaches of the river.

REGION 4
River Nene
Part of a complex drainage system, the Nene is one of three main rivers that run through the Fens to the Wash.

REGION 3
River Severn
The very high silt load carried by this river, which rises on Plynlimon in mid Wales, forms extensive salt marshes on reaching the estuary. The upper section of the Severn is rapid, while its lower reaches are slow-moving.

REGION 2
River Thames
The largest and most famous river in England is no longer in so much danger from pollution, thanks to stricter controls and a decline of industry in London. The river rises in the Cotswolds, and is generally slow moving. Its upper reaches are especially rich in wildlife, and are edged by meadows that harbour some of the rarest meadow flowers in Britain.

REGION 6
River Spey, Highland
Water from the north and west slopes of the Cairngorms drains into this fast-flowing Highland river. The estuary of Speymouth, 8 miles north-east of Elgin, is rich in coastal flora and birdlife.

REGION 2
Stour Estuary, Essex
This estuary, with its wide mudflats and salt marshes, is a popular bird-watching area. The best vantage points are on the south side of the estuary.

REGION 6
Tay Estuary, Tayside
Situated west of Dundee; access at Kingoodie and Port Allen. Reed-fringed marshes give way to extensive intertidal mudflats on the estuary and the sea birds and waterfowl that are attracted here have earned the area nationwide acclaim. Autumn visitors include large flocks of up to 20,000 pink-footed geese.

Directory

Given on these and the following pages are details of areas of the British countryside that are officially recognized as being either of outstanding beauty or scientific interest. There are also descriptions of 11 long distance paths, brief summaries of the public's rights in the countryside and the names and addresses of organizations concerned with all aspects of the countryside.

National Parks

The National Parks were created by Act of Parliament in the 1950s. They are areas of wild and beautiful countryside preserved for the nation. Each park is run by an executive committee drawn from members of the local authority and other interested organizations. This administrates the provision of such amenities as car parks, picnic sites and toilets, and provides information centres and the staff to care for the park. However, the land remains privately owned, either by individuals or by such bodies as the Crown Estates or the Forestry Commission. Unless a local arrangement has been made, the public has no more rights of way in a National Park than anywhere else in the country, and must respect the fact that people work and live in the Parks.

In Scotland, the scale and beauty of the countryside merits virtually the whole country being created a National Park, but this is obviously impractical, and less necessary, as the countryside is under far less threat from overcrowding than that south of the border. Instead, Scotland has five National Park Direction Area Orders covering countryside of exceptional beauty which may be under some risk. These areas are Loch Lomond and the Trossachs; Glen Affric, Glen Cannich and Strathfarrar; Ben Nevis, Glen Coe and Black Mount; the Cairngorms, Loch Torridon, Loch Maree and Little Loch Broom. Any proposals for development in these areas must be submitted to the Countryside Commission for Scotland, which advises the Secretary of State for Scotland on their acceptability.

Brecon Beacons: 579 square miles of mountain, moorland and pastoral farming countryside. The towns of Hay-on-Wye, Abergavenny, Brynamman, Llandeilo and Brecon lie within, or very close to the park. The Brecon Beacons themselves rise to almost 3,000 ft, their slopes often bracken-covered, the sandstone beneath in places eroded away by streams and rivers to create spectacular gorges. By contrast, the park also contains 31 miles of the Monmouthshire and Brecon Canal.

Dartmoor: the park covers 365 square miles of some of the wildest country left in southern England. There are 30,000 acres of peat bog, conifer plantations, broad-leaved woods along the river valleys and miles of heather broken only by occasional outcrops of granite known as tors. Buzzards, a few merlins, ravens, ring ouzels, stonechats and wheatears breed on the moorland; adders and lizards live in the heather; and unusual plants, such as the sundew, may be found in the boggy areas.

Exmoor: superb heather moorland, a magnificent coastline and a gentle countryside of patchwork fields are the three contrasting landscapes found within these 265 square miles which lie mainly in Somerset but also cover a little of north-west Devon. The park's red deer are a particular attraction for the naturalist.

Lake District: England's highest mountains and largest lakes lie within this park of 866 square miles in Cumbria. The famous limestone countryside, craggy and precipitous, supports a varied flora and fauna, including rare alpine plants only found clinging to crevices thousands of feet above sea level, and the spectacular peregrine falcon.

Northumberland: a remote 398 square miles between the Scottish border and Hadrian's Wall, with desolate but beautiful landscapes including the heather-clad sandstone Simonside Hills and the round-topped Cheviots. The Forestry Commission has some plantations of conifers here; otherwise there is only the occasional valley or fast-flowing mountain stream to break up the bare landscape.

North York Moors: 553 square miles largely made up of undulating heather moorland, the largest tract in England. The spectacular coast includes Robin Hood's Bay and the charming fishing village of Staithes. Inland, the moors become saturated with colour in August when the heather blooms.

Peak District: this was the first of Britain's National Parks, and covers 542 square miles, mostly in Derbyshire but also taking up parts of Staffordshire, Cheshire, South and West Yorkshire. There are two principal landscapes; in the north the grim gritstone Dark Peak, which includes the peat wilderness of Kinder Scout; and in the south the gentler limestone country of the White Peak, cut by wooded dales and fine trout-fishing rivers.

Pembrokeshire Coast: the smallest of the National Parks, but perhaps one of the most beautiful. For naturalists, botanists and geologists this coastline is richly rewarding, and fascinating for historians. Skomer Island, home of puffins, razorbills and Manx shearwaters, is part of the park, as are parts of the Preseli Hills inland.

Snowdonia: eight mountain ranges lie within the 838 square miles of the park. The mountainous countryside is among the wildest and most majestic in the British Isles. The park also includes part of the north Wales coast from Aberdyfi to just north of Harlech. Several nature reserves within the park include habitats as various as oakwoods, beaches and precipitous mountain sides.

Yorkshire Dales: a park of 680 square miles with the towns of Skipton, Settle, Sedbergh and Richmond on its borders, this is an area of high, bare fell in the central Pennines. Hewn out of the moorland are long narrow valleys, sheltered and green, in which villages have grown beside clear-running streams. In sharp contrast to the valleys are the inhospitable moors, where grouse are perhaps the most numerous living things apart from sheep.

Areas of Outstanding Natural Beauty

Complementing the National Park system, Areas of Outstanding Natural Beauty are large areas of beautiful countryside not large or wild enough to merit National Park status. There are 33 such areas in England and Wales so far, covering about 5,600 square miles. Unlike National Parks they have no special administration or facilities for public recreation. In Scotland the equivalent of the AONB is a National Scenic Area, of which there are about 40 designated so far, often in wild and remote parts of the Scottish countryside. Listed below are the more accessible AONBs of England and Wales; for further information about these contact the Countryside Commission, and for those in Scotland, the Countryside Commission for Scotland.

Anglesey: 84 square miles – almost the entire island, which lies off the coast of north Wales. A lowland landscape in miniature.

Arnside and Silverdale: limestone country at the southern tip of the Lake District National Park overlooking Morecambe Bay.

Cannock Chase: heathland and woods near Stafford. This is an area of 26 square miles, part of which is free from traffic.

Chichester Harbour: 29 square miles of harbour and estuary featuring extensive salt marshes; many seabirds and small waders.

The Chilterns: the well-known chalk hills of Oxfordshire, Buckinghamshire, Hertfordshire and Bedfordshire. Fine walking country renowned for its downland and splendid beech woods.

Cornwall: the AONB covers the county's finer areas – chiefly coast but also considerable chunks of inland countryside, including Bodmin Moor.

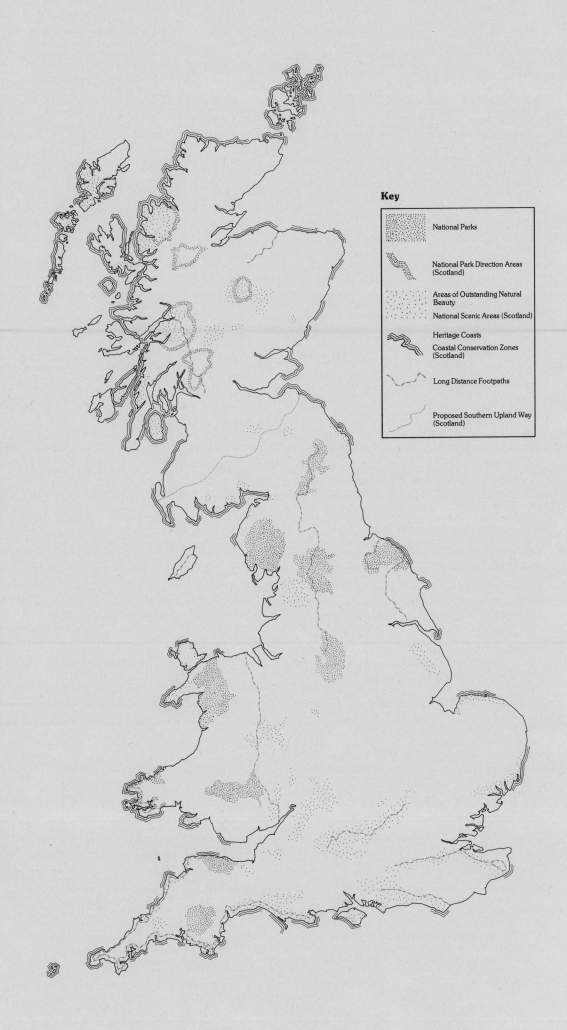

Key

▓ National Parks

◇ National Park Direction Areas (Scotland)

∴ Areas of Outstanding Natural Beauty
National Scenic Areas (Scotland)

〰 Heritage Coasts
Coastal Conservation Zones (Scotland)

⋯ Long Distance Footpaths

⋯ Proposed Southern Upland Way (Scotland)

The Cotswolds: perhaps the area which is held as most typically English because of the rolling, rich countryside and the beautiful stone-built villages. 582 square miles between Bath, Cheltenham and Cirencester.

Dedham Vale: a small area of 22 square miles including the countryside immortalized by Constable in his landscape paintings.

Dorset: virtually all the county's coastline and downland, comprising 400 square miles.

East Devon: 103 square miles adjacent to the Dorset AONB, and stretching westward as far as Exmouth. Inland are quaint villages and undulating farmland; along the splendid coast stand some of the cliffs of red sandstone for which Devon is famous.

East Hampshire: 161 square miles between Winchester and Petersfield, mostly fine downland scenery.

Forest of Bowland: 310 square miles of mostly open moorland in North Yorkshire and Lancashire.

The Gower: the first AONB, designated in 1956, this comprises 75 square miles on the peninsula west of Swansea. Unspoilt beaches, coves and sand dunes.

Isle of Wight: two thirds of the island is an AONB – beautiful beaches backed by downs.

Kent Downs: classic chalk downland scenery of 326 square miles between Orpington and Dover.

Lincolnshire Wolds: deserted chalk hills which run parallel to the coast but ten miles inland. Surrounded by flat country, partly fenland.

Lleyn: 60 square miles of the Lleyn peninsula is designated an AONB, an area unchanged and apparently timeless, which stretches out into the Irish Sea. Much gorse, bracken and rough pasture seemingly forgotten by modern agricultural practice.

Mendip Hills: typical limestone scenery between Weston-super-Mare and the city of Wells, with views over the Bristol Channel. In this area are the famous attractions of Wookey Hole and Cheddar Gorge.

Malvern Hills: with several summits over 1,000 ft high giving magnificent views, yet easily accessible, this AONB of 40 square miles covering parts of Gloucestershire, Herefordshire and Worcestershire, is extremely popular yet still capable of instilling a sense of solitude in the visitor.

Norfolk Coast: 174 square miles of beaches, mud flats and salt marsh between King's Lynn and Mundesley. A valuable habitat for coastal flora, insects and birds, especially wading species.

North Devon: rugged coastline from the county boundary with Cornwall to the Exmoor National Park.

Northumberland Coast: includes Holy Island and the Farne Islands. An unspoilt coast – the intemperate climate tends to discourage the traditional holidaymaker from the beaches along this stretch between Amble and Berwick-on-Tweed.

North Wessex Downs: 671 square miles of Hampshire, Wiltshire, Oxfordshire and Berkshire. This is the least spoiled of the chalk downlands in southern England.

Quantock Hills: a range of hills in Somerset running north of Taunton to Watchet on the coast. Wooded valleys and bracken-clad hills.

Scilly Isles: an archipelago 30 miles off Land's End, the Scilly Isles are washed by the Gulf Stream. Excellent marine and seashore wild-life, colourful sub-tropical flora, and an important landfall for migrating birds in spring and autumn, when rare species are recorded nearly every year.

Shropshire Hills: 300 square miles of the high hills south of Shrewsbury, some of which rise to 1,800 ft.

Solway Coast: the AONB stretches from Maryport in Cumbria to the Scottish border, covering 41 square miles of mostly flat country, with fine beaches overlooking the Solway Firth.

South Devon: 128 square miles between Plymouth and Torbay. Beautiful coastal scenery extremely popular with holidaymakers, but still there are secluded estuaries and inlets where wildlife remains undisturbed.

South Hampshire Coast: the AONB covers the coast south of the New Forest, from Beaulieu to west of Lymington.

Suffolk Coast and Heaths: an area of flat land between the Orwell estuary and Ipswich – 150 square miles threaded by wooded estuaries and numerous creeks, providing an ideal habitat for wildfowl.

Surrey Hills: 160 square miles of chalk downland and greensand from Haslemere and Farnham to Kent. The greensand hills offer a contrast in vegetation – silver birch and bracken, and also views across the Weald.

The Sussex Downs: chalk hills, covering 379 square miles, with views to the north across the Weald and to the coast southwards.

Long-distance footpaths

The paths described below have been officially adopted, and are approved by the Secretary of State for the Environment.

The Cleveland Way: a 100-mile path which skirts the North Yorks National Park from Helmsley to Saltburn, from where it crosses outstanding coastal scenery to Filey – a stretch defined as Heritage Coast by the Countryside Commission. The inland path, much of it over moorland, offers a wealth of historic remains from the barely discernible ramparts of Iron-Age forts to the majestic ruins of the Norman Rievaulx Abbey. The coastal path takes in cliff-top paths and walks at beach level – which strengthen the extraordinary contrast found between the two specialized wild life habitats of the seashore and the high heather moorland.

Wolds Way: the newest of the long-distance footpaths, the Wolds Way is a southern extension of the Cleveland Way. It stretches 67 miles from Filey to North Ferriby across the Lincolnshire Wolds – a landscape of rolling hills, deep valleys and beech hangers. The area is fairly sparsely populated, but it is one of England's most prosperous farming areas where fields of wheat stretch from horizon to horizon, and peas are grown for frozen-food companies.

North Downs Way: a very convenient walk for Londoners – as it begins at Farnham railway station on the Waterloo line. The 141-mile-long path is never far from a railway station along its entire length, which makes it easy to walk in sections. The path finishes at Shakespeare Cliff near Dover, where the North Downs meet the Channel.

Offa's Dyke Path: from near the Severn Bridge to Prestatyn in north Wales this path follows roughly the line of the 8th-century earthwork built by the King of Mercia, who wished to define the boundary between his lands and those of the Welsh. In the choice of route, scenery was the guiding factor, so in many places the 168-mile-long walk parts company with Offa's Dyke. The path follows the beautiful Wye Valley, visits Tintern Abbey, White Castle, the Black Mountains, Hay-on-Wye and eventually the Clwydian Hills. Scenery along the path includes lush valleys, bare 2,000 ft-high ridges and ancient deciduous woodlands.

The Pembrokeshire Coast Path: virtually all of this 168-mile-long path falls within the Pembrokeshire Coast National Park. The constantly changing seascapes are as varied as the wildlife for which the coast is famous. Wild flowers grow in profusion and bloom early, and the area is one of Britain's richest for seabirds and seals. The path runs round the Pembrokeshire peninsula from Tenby to Cardigan.

The Pennine Way: the most famous and the most difficult of the long-distance footpaths, the Pennine Way runs 270 miles from Edale in the Peak District to Kirk Yetholm in Scotland. The scenery is wild along much of the path, and as it follows the limestone backbone of the Pennines, the flora is sub-alpine. To walk the path from end to end is a challenge for the most experienced fell walker – the steep climbs, peat bogs, featureless moorland and the possibility of encountering foul weather without warning are not to be undertaken lightly. It passes through both the Yorkshire Dales and Northumberland National Parks.

The Ridgeway: the path begins on the 800ft-high summit of Ivinghoe Beacon near Ivinghoe village, and traverses 85 miles of countryside to Overton Hill near Avebury. The scenery alternates between glorious beechwoods, wide-open downland and cosy, well-kept farmland. It is one of the easiest of the long-distance footpaths, along which the countryside has been largely shaped by man over the centuries to suit his own purposes. It follows the prehistoric Ridgeway path for about half its length, and passes close to some of the finest prehistoric remains in the country.

The South Downs Way: this footpath is also a bridleway, and is open to riders, cyclists and walkers along its entire length except for the alternative walk along the cliff-tops of the Seven Sisters at the coastal end. The 80 miles of public right of way falls within the Sussex Downs Area of Outstanding Natural Beauty, beginning at Eastbourne and finishing at the West Sussex/Hampshire border near Petersfield. Wild flowers, butterflies and birds abound on the chalk downs, and it is easy walking on the short downland turf along this ancient route.

The South West Peninsula Coast Path: this is made up of four coastal paths, which together account for a footpath 572 miles long. The path begins at Minehead in Somerset, and finishes, via Land's End, at Poole in Dorset. Staying as close as possible to the coast, whether cliffs, beaches, dunes or estuary, it visits some of Britain's finest coastal scenery and several of the country's prettiest villages. Wild flowers are abundant owing to the mild climate, and seabirds of many species are likely to be encountered along the way. The four separate coastal paths are: the Dorset Coast Path (74 miles); the South Devon Coast Path (93 miles); the Cornwall Coast Path (267 miles) and the Somerset and North Devon Coastal Path (81 miles).

The Speyside Way: the Way runs for 60 miles from Glenmore Lodge near Aviemore to Spey Bay on the Moray Firth. The path passes through varied countryside as it climbs from the coastal plain to the Grampians, following the course of the salmon-bearing River Spey. This path has only just been completed.

The West Highland Way: this was the first long-distance footpath designated in Scotland. It runs for 95 miles from Milngavie on the outskirts of Glasgow northwards to Fort William. It passes through Highland and Lowland scenery, the Way becoming progressively more difficult to walk as it presses northwards. In the Highlands it follows old drove roads and military roads of the 18th century, and farm tracks and old coaching routes in the Lowland stretches. Outstanding features along the route are Loch Lomond, Scotland's largest loch, and Ben Nevis, Scotland's highest mountain.

Sites of Special Scientific Interest
There are 3,356 SSSIs designated in Great Britain. These are usually small pieces of land, privately owned, which are particularly valuable for their geology or natural history. A landowner whose property includes a SSSI must notify the Nature Conservancy Council of any development that is intended for that area. Those interested in finding out more about these sites should contact the Nature Conservancy Council or their local county naturalists' trust.

Nature Reserves
By Act of Parliament there are over 250 national nature reserves in Great Britain, some 164 run by the Nature Conservancy Council, others by local authorities. Nature reserves are also set up by private organizations, such as the Royal Society for the Protection of Birds, who have 77 reserves, and by county naturalists' trusts. Those reserves created by Act of Parliament are often freely open to the public, others, however, require a visitor to apply for a special permit.

Heritage Coasts
One of Britain's most valuable national assets is the quality and variety of her coastlines. The coast, however, is also the most popular holiday destination, and consequently there are conflicts between the needs of conservation and recreation. In an effort to conserve and define the most beautiful and unspoilt stretches of coast, these have been designated Heritage Coasts. Those areas so far defined are marked on the map on page 117. In Scotland Coastal Conservation Zones take the place of Heritage Coasts.

The Law and the Countryside
Every inch of Britain is owned by somebody, and to wander from public rights of way without permission is bound to be an act of trespass. However, there is sufficient legal access to make this unnecessary throughout most of the countryside – and where there is not, ask permission from the landowner and remember that if he refuses you access he probably has a very good reason. There is no need for conflict between visitor and local; the countryside can be enjoyed by all provided they obey the basic laws of the land and follow the Country Code.

The Country Code
Enjoy the countryside and respect its life and work
Guard against all risk of fire
Fasten all gates
Keep dogs under close control
Keep to public paths across farmland
Use gates and stiles to cross fences, hedges and walls
Leave livestock, crops and machinery alone
Take your litter home
Help to keep all water clean
Protect wildlife, plants and trees
Take special care on country roads
Make no unnecessary noise

Footpaths and bridleways
County councils and the Ordnance Survey publish maps on which footpaths and bridleways are marked as public rights of way. On a bridleway the public may ride or cycle as well as walk. All land belongs to someone, and although footpaths may grant rights of way over private land, there are restrictions. A walker may rest, but not wander from the footpath or picnic unless the landowner does not object. Plants and animals must be left alone. If a walker does stray from the footpath without permission he is liable to be accused of trespass. A trespasser can be sued for civil damages even if he has caused no physical damage. If there is damage to crops, trees, animals or property, he can be prosecuted in a criminal court. Similarly he can be prosecuted for trespass with a firearm, or if he removes cultivated plants or fruit. Picking wild flowers is an act of trespass. Farmers on the other hand can plough over a footpath if it crosses an established field, although the right of way still exists and the field can be crossed. The farmer has to make good the paths within a given period. Landowners are responsible,

however, for the repair of stiles and gates along the footpath, and cannot obstruct the right of way. Highway authorities must provide signposts to footpaths and bridleways where they leave a metalled road, except where a parish council agrees a signpost is unnecessary.

Commons and Village Greens
Rights of Common are enjoyed by some local people over land on which certain rights are shared – such as fishing, taking peat for fuel or collecting wood. Common land is shown on maps kept by the local county council, and people with rights over the land are registered under the 1965 Commons Registration Act. The public does not necessarily have any access over common land, but some commons are special exemptions. These are: commons within a borough or urban district; National Trust commons; commons managed by rural district councils; commons where the landowner has granted access; nationally important commons such as Ashdown Forest and the Malvern Hills.

Village greens are not necessarily common land, and may still be privately owned. The villagers, however, are granted the right to play games by a Local Enclosure Act or have the right through tradition.

Parking, Camping and Caravanning
It is wise only to park where it is authorized by local authorities. To obstruct a highway, by parking in a narrow country lane for example, is an offence, and to park on adjacent land without the owner's consent is trespass. There are also special cases – it is an offence to park on a borough or urban district common, and there are often other similar restrictions created by local bye-laws for other areas which at first glance appear to be an ideal parking place for a picnic.

Seaside Rights
The public have a right to sail and fish the sea, and have right of navigation over the foreshore when it is covered by the tide, to estuaries and tidal rivers, although these are often subject to local bye-laws. Most of the foreshore in Britain belongs to the Crown Estate Commissioners, who allow public access to most of the coast. Above the high water mark the beach can be privately owned and fenced, and the public have no right of access unless there is a public right of way or a highway.

organizations concerned with all aspects of the countryside, and societies to join.

Association for the Preservation of Rural Scotland, 20 Falkland Avenue, Newton Mearns, G77 5DR. *Aims to protect the countryside and monitor legislation affecting it.*

Botanical Society of the British Isles, 68 Outwoods Road, Loughborough, Leicestershire. *Supports conservation of wild flowering plants and ferns.*

British Butterfly Conservation Society, Tudor House, Quorn, Leicestershire, LE12 8AD. *Promotes the conservation and study of butterflies.*

British Mountaineering Council, Crowford House, Precinct Centre, Booth Street East, Manchester, M13 9RZ. *Looks after the interests of British mountaineers, and deals with aspects of access and conservation of mountain areas.*

British Naturalists' Association, Willowfield, Boyneswood Road, Four Marks, Alton, Hants. *Provides support for maintenance and promotion of National Parks, nature reserves and conservation areas.*

British Speleological Association, 4 Kingston Avenue, Acklam, Middlesbrough, Cleveland, TS5 7RS. *Furthers the sport of caving and all aspects of caves in Britain.*

British Tourist Authority, 64 St James's Street, London. SW1A 1NF.

British Trust for Conservation Volunteers HQ, Zoological Gardens, Regent's Park, London, NW1 4RY. *Organizes volunteers willing to involve themselves in practical conservation.*

British Trust for Ornithology, Beech Grove, Tring, Herts. *Coordinates the work of British ornithologists and promotes the study of birds.*

British Waterways Board, Melbury House, Melbury Terrace, London, NW1 6JX. *Manages the nationalized inland waterways – some 2,000 miles of canals and navigable rivers.*

Camping Club of Great Britain & Ireland Ltd, 11 Lower Grosvenor Place, London, SW1 0EY.

Caravan Club, 65 South Molton Street, London, W1Y 2AB.

Civic Trust, 17 Carlton House Terrace, London, SW1 5 AW. *Promotes and assists in the improvement and preservation of the environment.*

Committee for Environmental Conservation (Co En Co), 29–31 Greville Street, London, EC1W 8AX. *Encourages ways of using natural resources economically, and a forum for the major conservation*

organizations to discuss major problems.

Commons, Open Spaces and Footpaths Preservation Society, 166 Shaftesbury Avenue, London, WC2H 8JH. *Concerned with the conservation of common land and village greens, and with preserving rights of access in the countryside.*

Conservation Society, 12 London Street, Chertsey, Surrey, KT16 8AA. *Aims to promote awareness of the limited extent of natural resources.*

Council for British Archaeology, 8 St Andrew's Place, Regents Park, London, NW1 4LB. *Provides information for people interested in helping in field work.*

Council for National Parks, 4 Hobart Place, London, SW1W 0HY. *Aims to preserve National Parks.*

Council for Nature, Zoological Gardens, Regent's Park, London, NW1 4RY. *National representative for the United Kingdom's natural historians. Has many associates and affiliations, such as with the county naturalists' trusts.*

Council for the Protection of Rural England (CPRE), 4 Hobart Place, London, SW1W 0HY. *Aims to improve the countryside, and monitor legislation which could affect it.*

Council for the Protection of Rural Wales, 14 Broad Street, Welshpool, Powys, SY21 7SD. *Similar to the CPRE.*

Country Landowners' Association, 16 Belgrave Square, London, SW1X 8PQ. *Association which represents landowners in England and Wales.*

Countryside Commission, John Dower House, Crescent Place, Cheltenham, Glos, GL50 3RA. *The official body concerned with the countryside. Among its functions is the designation of national parks, AONBs and other conservation areas.*

Countryside Commission for Scotland, Battleby, Redgarton, Perth, PH1 3EW. *Provides, develops and improves facilities for the enjoyment of the Scottish countryside.*

County Naturalists' Trusts, Royal Society for Nature Conservation, The Green, Nettleham, Lincoln, LN2 2NR. *Every county in England and Wales has an active naturalists' trust. The Royal Society for Nature Conservation coordinates their activities.*

Department of the Environment, 2 Marsham Street, London, SW1P 3EB. *The Government department which deals with environmental issues.*

Fauna Preservation Society, Zoological Society of London, Regent's Park, London, NW1 4RX. *A worldwide organization devoted to safeguarding wild animals and their habitats.*

Field Studies Council, Director and Information Office, Preston Montford, Montford Bridge, Shrewsbury, SY4 1HW. *Encourages fieldwork and study of all outdoors subjects.*

Forestry Commission HQ, 231 Corstophine Road, Edinburgh, EH12 7AT. London office: 25 Savile Row, London W1X 2AY. *A government agency concerned with timber production, but increasingly concerned with conservation and the provision of recreational facilities.*

Friends of the Earth, 9 Poland Street, London, W1V 3DG. *A pressure group founded in 1970 to promote understanding of the need for conservation.*

Greenpeace, Colombo Street, London, SE1 8DP. *An internationally active conservation organization well known for its demonstrations against whaling and nuclear power.*

Men of the Trees, Crawley Down, Crawley, Sussex. *Encourages the planting and preservation of trees.*

National Trust, 42 Queen Anne's Gate, London, SW1H 9AS. *Owns and preserves for the nation unspoiled countryside and coast, and also many historic buildings.*

National Trust for Scotland, 5 Charlotte Square, Edinburgh, EH2 4DV. *Aims similar to the National Trust.*

Nature Conservancy Council, 19/20 Belgrave Square, London, SW1X 8PY. *Establishes, maintains and manages National Nature Reserves, and advises generally on conservation.*

Otter Trust, Earsham, Near Bungay, Suffolk. *Promotes conservation and study of otters.*

Ramblers' Association, 123 Wandsworth Road, London, SW8 2LJ. *Protects interests of those who enjoy walking in the countryside.*

Royal Society for the Protection of Birds HQ, The Lodge, Sandy, Bedfordshire, SG19 2BL. *Protects and conserves wild birds in Britain. Owns and manages over 70 reserves throughout the country.*

Scottish Field Studies Council, Forelands, 18 Marketgate, Crail, Fife, KY10 3TL. *Aims similar to those of the Field Studies Council.*

Scottish Rights of Way Society, 32 Rutland Square, Edinburgh, EH1 2BZ. *Preserves, defends and acquires public rights of way in Scotland.*

Scottish Tourist Board, 2 Rutland Place, Edinburgh, EH1 1YU.

Scottish Wildlife Trust, 8 Dublin Street, Edinburgh, EH1 3PP. *Seeks to prevent destruction of wildlife and habitats in Scotland.*

The Soil Association, Walnut Tree Manor, Houghley, Stowmarket, Suffolk, IP14 3RS. *Campaigns for organic husbandry as an alternative to modern, orthodox farming.*

Society for the Protection of Ancient Buildings, 55 Great Ormond Street, London, WC1 N3J. *Seeks to preserve buildings of historic or architectural interest.*

Society for the Promotion of Nature Reserves, The Manor House, Aldford, Lincolnshire. *Promotes conservation, study and appreciation of nature, and establishes and manages nature reserves.*

Tree Council, 35 Belgrave Square, London, SW1X 8QN. *Promotes the planting and cultivation of trees in Britain.*

Watch, c/o Royal Society for Nature Conservation, 22 The Green, Nettleham, Lincoln. *Educates young people in the understanding and appreciation of nature.*

Water Space Amenity Commission, 1 Queen Anne's Gate, London, SW1H 9BT. *Links interests of the Water Board and those of public recreation.*

Wild Flower Society, Rams Hill House, Horsmonden, Tonbridge, Kent.

Wildfowl Trust, The New Grounds, Slimbridge, Glos, GL2 7BT. *Concerned with the study of wildfowl and their conservation.*

Wildlife Youth Service of the World Wildlife Fund, Wildlife, Wallington, Surrey. *Encourages the young to take an active part in nature conservation.*

Woodland Trust, Westgate, Grantham, Lincolnshire, NG31 6LL. *Conserves and seeks to re-establish trees and all other plants and wildlife in the United Kingdom.*

World Wildlife Fund, Panda House, 29 Greville Street, London, EC1N 8AX. *International organization which raises money for conserving and safeguarding animals and plants in danger of extinction.*

Things to do and What to take

The British countryside offers unending pleasures and great variety. These pleasures and experiences are free to all who enter the countryside with patience, care and the desire to learn. Both the pleasures and the rewards can be enriched with the help of some basic pieces of equipment and some ideas of what to look for.

Watching wildlife

There are few things more exciting when in the countryside than to be able to watch wild creatures at close quarters. The most important skill necessary in order to watch any creature, whether it be fox or ant, is patience. On a country ramble all kinds of birds and animals might be glimpsed, but they are usually seen as they run away or make for cover. Crickets, for example, spend most of their time on bright summer days basking on the top of leaves, but when approached they quickly move to the underside of the leaf. Those with the patience to wait will be rewarded when, after a minute or two, the cricket returns to its sunny seat.

The best way to observe the natural comings and goings in the countryside is to find a quiet spot and sit down. For a few minutes nothing may happen, but presently the wild creatures will accept you as part of the scenery and continue about their business. There are a few simple tips that can help you blend into the surroundings more easily. Find a spot where you can sit without being conspicuous. Choose a place that is comfortable; your chances of seeing anything are greatly diminished if you are constantly shifting about to avoid a stone, brambles, or damp patch (it is often a good idea to take something waterproof to sit on). Wear clothes that blend with the surroundings – neutral greens and browns are best. There are exceptions to the clothing rule; those walking in mountains or moorland may wish to wear bright clothes which would attract attention in the event of them falling into difficulties.

Try to visit the same place many times. That way you will learn which are the best places to watch for wild creatures, for they usually keep to the same paths and places, and once these have been learned you will be able to return time and time again knowing that you stand a fair chance of seeing them.

However, there is a world of difference between watching wildlife and disturbing it. It should spoil your day if your presence unduly frightens or disturbs any creature, so try to learn a little woodcraft and move slowly, silently and carefully. If you constantly disturb any creature it will eventually move home, and it may desert a nest or its young. If you know that your presence disturbs a creature, then move away as quietly as possible.

Getting to know an area of countryside intimately has many rewards. You will see 'your patch' in all seasons and in all moods, and you will begin to notice more and more about the things around you. You may discover, perhaps, that the tree you had walked past many times thinking it was a kind of willow is actually a rare black poplar, or that the footpath you follow is an ancient parish boundary originally marked out in Anglo-Saxon times.

'Your patch' need not be a local beauty spot, in fact it may be better if it is an area disregarded by most. That way you are likely to have the natural world to yourself. Wild plants and creatures do not live in places because they are beautiful; they live in any available place that suits their requirements.

Binoculars

Although not essential, binoculars can greatly increase the pleasure derived from the countryside and its inhabitants. Choosing binoculars is very much a matter of personal taste, but bear in mind what you want to use them for, and that you probably want them to last a long time. Binoculars of every size, type, price and description are available, but the most expensive binoculars may not be the best for you, and the cheapest may not a bargain. If you intend to carry your binoculars for long periods, then you will not want a pair that are so heavy they become a burden.

Try out several binoculars before making a final choice. Check them for ease of use and be sure that they do not give a distorted image. Those with coated lenses give a better image. Check the specifications of the binoculars, and remember that those with the highest magnification may not give the best image; the important consideration is their light-gathering power. To discover this divide the object lens diameter by the magnification (these figures appear on the binoculars as 7×50, or 8×40, etc). If the figure is more than 5 (in the case of 7×50 it is 7) then the light-gathering potential is satisfactory. The reason for this is that on a bright day in the open, binoculars with low light-gathering power may work very well, but on dull days or in woodland they will give a murky image.

Try to prevent your binoculars getting wet, since water may enter them and cause corrosion or misting of the lenses and prisms. The prisms are easily moved out of alignment if the binoculars receive a hard knock, and this may result in a double image that only an optician will be able to rectify. It is usually wise to have the binocular strap round your neck at all times – otherwise they might end up in the sea or at the bottom of a hill.

Hand lens

A magnifying or hand lens is another piece of equipment that is not essential but can greatly increase the pleasure and knowledge gained from the natural world. Through a hand lens the intricate patterns on a fly's wing can be seen, and the wonderful colouring of a butterfly's wing will take on a new significance. All flowers look lovelier through a lens, and some flowers and plants can be accurately identified only through a close examination of their features.

Notebooks

You will not always have a field guide or reference book handy when you want to identify a particular animal or plant. In such cases a small book in which you can make notes can be invaluable. Hard-backed books with plain pages are best. For writing and sketches pencils are better than pens since they do not dry up or leak, and pencil lead will not smudge the pages. Pencils also enable much subtler and more accurate drawings to be made.

If you want to record a bird that you wish to identify, draw it (a work of art is not necessary) and also write down as many details as possible: where you saw it, what it was doing, time of day, its size, shape, coloration and all distinguishing features. Such notes made on the spot are always more accurate than memory.

Notebooks can also help you to see. Try writing down the name of every species of plant that you see on a walk, and you will probably be surprised how many species this simple exercise reveals.

Keeping a detailed nature diary is a natural extension of the notebook idea. After you have returned from a walk or outing write down all that you have seen. Not only will this give you a record that you can refer back to, it will also help you to be more objective about your experiences.

Accurate records of the natural world can be of tremendous help to organizations like the British Trust for Ornithology. Such organizations will be pleased to send details of the kinds of records they require (for some addresses see pages 120–121).

Identification books

There is now an immense number of books available covering every aspect of the British countryside. For on-the-spot use, books that fit in the pocket and do not weigh too much are obviously the best. There is a wide choice of these available, ranging from tiny books costing very little to the fat 'field guides'. Choosing such books is of course a matter of personal taste, but be sure that the book suits your requirements and does its job well. Often this can only be discovered when the book is used, but ask like-minded friends which books they use, and make sure the book has good illustrations, clear text and is easy to use. A lavish book is of no use if it is organized in such a way that you have no idea where to look in it for the thing that you wish to identify.

Maps and libraries

Maps can do a very great deal more than show you where you are. They can provide a tremendous amount of information about the living countryside, and give clues to the past. The Ordnance Survey's 1 : 50,000 series shows all the detail necessary for day-to-day use, but the 1 : 25,000 series is invaluable for a closer inspection of a particular area. Maps at even larger scales have been produced, but they are not usually generally available. They may, however, be held in public libraries.

Public libraries are an invaluable source of reference for the naturalist and historian. Current Ordnance Survey maps are usually held in the reference section of libraries, and editions of old maps may also be available. These can be fascinating and informative documents which reveal a tremendous amount about the past of particular areas of countryside. They may, perhaps, reveal where a lane that now peters out in the middle of a field once led, or show that a tiny patch of trees was once part of a much larger wood. Even older maps, and other ancient documents, may be held by your local county archivist.

History in the countryside

While maps and reference books are invaluable, and essential, for discovering the history of the countryside, the initial, and perhaps most exciting, work is done on the ground.

The age of hedgerows, for example, can be worked out roughly by counting the number of tree and shrub species (excluding climbers like ivy and honeysuckle) in a 30-yard stretch. It has been calculated that hedges gain about one new species every century, so if there are three species in a 30-yard stretch the hedge is probably about 300 years old, and if there are nine, the hedge may have been established before the Norman Conquest. You should not start to count species near the ends of a hedge, since these are more likely to have been influenced by adjacent woodlands and other factors, nor should you wander up and down the hedge until you find a stretch that looks particularly rich in species; the count should be started at a random point along the hedge. Only one side of the hedge should be counted. The results that you gain may be accurate to within 200 years either way, but subsequent research at your library or in the offices of your local county archivist may enable you to arrive at a much more precise date.

It may also be possible to trace some of the history of a patch of woodland, since until fairly recently most deciduous woods were carefully managed, and men have inevitably left the marks of their work on the ground. Perhaps the first step is to find a fallen or felled tree and count its annual rings. You will probably find that gnarled old coppiced trees and pollards are far older than the tall 'standard' trees (for more details of these terms see pages 42–43). Ancient woods tend to be tucked away in remote corners of parishes, and often have irregular outlines to their boundaries. Many woods have bank-and-ditch earthworks marking their boundaries, and the shape of these can give a clue as to when they were excavated. As a general rule, ancient banks will have broad bases and rounded profiles, while more recent banks (and they were still being thrown up in the 19th century) will have a triangular profile and will probably occur in straight lines rather than curves. The species of plants and trees in a wood can also give clues to its history.

Many other landscape features can be examined in similar ways to give clues to their history and age. The principal prehistoric and Roman sites in Britain are well documented, and their location can usually be discovered by studying an Ordnance Survey map, or from one of the many excellent guides that can be obtained from library or bookshop.

History in the garden

Gardens which have been tended for a long time can be treasure-houses of small objects lost, or more likely thrown away, by previous tenants. Most often the objects that the spade turns up – bits of clay pipe, scraps of pottery, unidentifiable lumps of metal, the odd coin – are Victorian or later, but very occasionally they may be older.

The stems of clay pipes are commonly found. Much more exciting are their bowls. These come in a great variety of shapes and often have designs or patterns on them. Sometimes the date and the makers' name is stamped on. Clay pipe bowls of which the rims are not parallel with the stems are 17th-century or earlier.

Pottery finds include the easily broken parts of ornaments, like heads and limbs, and sometimes the tiny limbs of children's toys. Bottles are common finds in old garden sheds. Usually they are of no great age, but the details on them can be fascinating reminders of the past.

Wildlife in the garden

A surprising variety of wildlife can be attracted to gardens, even small ones, by the addition of a few features and by encouraging certain plants.

One of the most simple and effective attractions in any garden is a pond. This can be small, perhaps no more than two feet across, and can be constructed either of concrete or polythene. (Successful ponds have also been made of such things as old baths.) It should be at least 15 inches deep at its deepest point, and it should have sloping sides so that creatures like newts and frogs can get in and out easily. It should also be shallow enough in parts for birds to be able to bathe in it, and ideally it should have an island or two, constructed perhaps from bricks or stones, on which birds can perch.

Birds can be attracted to the garden by providing them with food to eat and suitable nesting sites. Shrubs that bear berries will attract a great many birds. Among the best are hawthorn, holly and yew. If your garden is not large enough for shrubs or trees then try to leave a bit of the garden wild, allowing such plants as thistles and docks to grow and set seed, since these will attract birds like goldfinches. If the garden has no suitable nesting sites, then nest boxes can be introduced. These can be either purchased complete, or made from scratch (a leaflet available from the British Trust for Ornithology gives details of several varieties and methods of construction). Nest boxes should be placed in positions where they are out of the reach of predators like cats, and they should not be placed where the full light of the sun beats down on them, since this is likely to result in boiled eggs or suffocated young.

A great many birds can be attracted to bird tables in the winter months. As a general rule, food should not be put out to birds during summer, since at that time there will be plenty of natural food available, and also because parent birds may try to feed bird-table food to baby birds, and such food may be indigestible by their tiny stomachs, causing pain and sometimes death.

Bird tables should be high enough to be out of the reach of predators, and they should also be well clear of trees and buildings from which cats could launch themselves at the birds. Ideally, bird tables should have a roof of some sort to keep the worst of the weather off the food, and the food tray should have drain holes in it to prevent the food becoming waterlogged.

A patch of ground allowed to grow wild in the garden will attract insects as well as birds. The caterpillars of several species of butterflies feed on stinging nettles, and some moth

caterpillars feed on dandelions. Several species of night-flying moth are attracted to bladder campion. Spiders will lurk in the foliage in a wild part of the garden, as will crickets and grasshoppers. Adult butterflies and moths will be attracted to gardens in which flowers like aubretia, phlox, honesty, tobacco plants and alyssum grow. The best-known of the butterfly-attracting plants is buddleia, which may be visited by a great variety of species. The ice plant comes into flower after the buddleia fades, and this flower will also attract large numbers of butterflies.

Compost heaps, especially loose ones under hedges, can support an astonishing variety of creatures, ranging from thousands of tiny invertebrates to mice, slow-worms and hedgehogs.

Sick or hurt animals and birds

Occasionally birds and animals are found which are either sick or injured. If the creature is so badly injured that it is obviously suffering or has no chance of survival, the kindest action is to kill it as quickly and humanely as possible. But a word of warning: all animals hang on to life tenaciously and an inexperienced or squeamish person can easily make the sufferings of the creature even more acute, as well as turning the business into a nightmare for himself. If there is any doubt the creature should be taken to the nearest vet or RSPCA official. If a creature is discovered which stands some chance of survival you may wish to try to help it recover. But to undertake such a task is a responsibility which involves time and patience. Once again, the best action is to seek advice from a vet, RSPCA official or other knowledgeable person.

Baby animals and birds are frequently encountered, and the general rule with these is to leave them alone. Parent birds or animals are usually very close, and will return to their young once you have moved on. Do not be tempted to pick up or stroke the baby creature; by doing so you will be transferring your scent to it and the parent may desert it for that reason.

If you are sure that the baby

creature has been deserted, then you may wish to help it, but once again it is advisable to seek help from an expert. Many baby birds, for example, are fed with food that has already been partly digested by the parent, so trying to force worms into their beaks is futile, since the young bird can neither swallow it properly nor digest it. If you do take on the responsibility of a baby creature you will be in for a great deal of hard work, but also great pleasure if it survives and thrives. You must always remember that the creature must not be taken or kept as a pet – you should look after it solely in order to be able to return it to the wild. On the other hand, a creature that has not had the benefit of its parent teaching it how to survive in the wild stands little or no chance if it is simply left in the countryside one day. You will need patience and knowledge to equip the creature for adult life, and you will probably also need the help and advice of an expert to prepare it for its life in the wild.

A day in the country

If you intend to spend a day in the country you should go properly equipped. Take something to drink, and plenty of food (oranges, apples, fruit cake and chocolate make excellent energy-providing snacks). Always wear stout shoes if you plan to do a lot of walking. Wellingtons are excellent for muddy or wet conditions, but they soon become hot and uncomfortable on a warm day. They are not suitable for really long walks, and can be positively dangerous if any scrambling across rocks is involved. It is always advisable to carry a warm jumper and waterproofs in your rucksack, since the British weather can change very quickly. This is especially so on moors and mountains. If you plan a day in wild countryside you should carry a map and compass (the *Silva* type is probably the best) and you should know how to use them. Always let someone know where you are going before you set out. Warnings can sound melodramatic, but each year a number of people die in the countryside because they either failed to take simple precautions or did not use their common sense.

Index

Acknowledgements

The publishers gratefully acknowledge the following for the use of photographs:

Aerofilms
Heather Angel
ARDEA
Automobile Association Publications Division Photographic Library
BIOFOTOS
British Tourist Authority
Robert Eames
Bob Johnson
Mansell Collection
Massey-Ferguson
Richard Newton
PRESS-TIGE Pictures
Wildlife Picture Agency (Leslie Jackman, Mike Leach, David Cayless)

Picture research by Sally Howard